sona
BOOKS

CAT NO. SON0597

Written by

Alice Pattillo

April Madden

Bee Ginger

Catherine Curzon

Joanna Elphick

Kate Puttick

Steve Wright

Proof reader: Juliette O'Neill

Images courtesy of

Alamy

Getty Images

Shutterstock

© Creative Commons/ArniEin

© Creative Commons/Sergey Krasilnikov

© Creative Commons/ Tadeáš Bednarz

Photographs: All copyrights and trademarks are recognised and respected

Made in EU.

ISBN: 978-1-915343-54-3

The Complete Beginner's Guide to

CRYSTALS

Welcome

Crystals have been enchanting the lives of millions of people for thousands of years. These stunning rocks are one of nature's most prized possessions, and we go above and beyond to unearth them. Whether you are enticed by their mysticism and interested in the metaphysical properties of the stones or simply enjoy the beauty they provide, *The Complete Beginner's Guide to Crystals* is a comprehensive guide to the history, science and myths surrounding gemstones. Learn how to identify them, which shapes best suit your intended uses and how our ancestors harnessed their ancient wisdom in order to enrich their everyday lives.

Plus, put your new found knowledge into practise by following our step-by-steps to enrich your own life – from healing and self care rituals to gridding and spellwork.

sona
BOOKS

CONTENTS

Introduction

10
Discovering crystals

12
How they work

14
Types of crystal

18
How to choose
your crystals

20
How to care
for your crystals

22
Crystal Gridding

28
Essential crystals
for your collection

Health

40
An introduction to
crystal healing

44
Chakras

48
How to heal
with crystals

52
Crystals for your health

Home

64

Displaying your crystals

·

72

Protecting your home

·

76

Crystals for family
& relationships

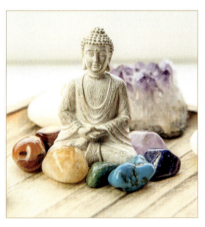

Lifestyle

84

Living with crystals

·

90

Crystals for self-care

·

98

Crystals for work

·

100

Travelling with crystals

Magic

104

The magic of crystals

·

106

Harnessing crystals to
get what you want

·

114

Stars & stones

·

120

What is divination?

Introduction

10

Discovering crystals

·

12

How crystals work

·

14

Types of crystal

·

18

How to choose your crystals

·

20

How to care for your crystals

·

22

Crystal gridding

·

28

Essential crystals for
your collection

Discovering
CRYSTALS

How and why crystals have fascinated us for centuries

Glittering, colourful stones have charmed us since ancient times and still do today. The earliest civilisation known to have decorated themselves, their homes and their sacred spaces with minerals was ancient Sumer, in modern-day Iraq. Their favourite stone was deep blue lapis lazuli, which to them represented the perfect sky of a cloudless day. Lapis lazuli wasn't found in their part of the world; they had to set up a long and extensive trade route with what is now Afghanistan to get their hands on the precious resource. It wasn't the only stone they used: a figurine of Inanna, the most powerful goddess of their pantheon and the one they believed had restored the lapis-blue skies to them after a terrifying flood-rain, is made of alabaster and gold, her eyes and belly button inset with rose-pink rubies.

The ancient Egyptians also used crystals and gemstones, not only as jewellery and objects but ground up into cosmetics too. Their eyelids were painted with green malachite, sacred to the goddess Wadjet (her name means 'the green one'), which was believed to protect them from the evil eye. They lined their eyes with kohl, made from stibnite – the raw material for the metalloid antimony. The dark paint had the added benefit of cutting down the reflected glare when looking out across the sun-shimmering desert, making it easier to see.

By the time of the ancient Greeks, the use of minerals and gemstones was well established. It's the ancient Greeks that gave us the distinction between precious and semi-precious stones. The first, referred to as gems or jewels, are rubies, sapphires, emeralds and diamonds. Every other kind of gemstone is referred to as semi-precious, and is often called a crystal, from the ancient Greek 'krustallos', which means both 'ice' and 'rock crystal', or quartz.

These semi-precious gemstones are more commonly found than precious stones, which has made them more widely available, and consequently less expensive, since ancient times. They're no less beautiful though, and capture the imagination just as much as their more valuable cousins. According to myth, the Greek god of wine, Dionysus, was once pursuing a nymph called Amethyst; she prayed to be turned into stone rather than face his amorous attentions. Surprised at finding his prospective

"Ancient Greeks gave us the distinction between precious and semi-precious stones"

lover petrified, Dionysus spilled his wine. When it hit Amethyst's crystalline form, it became the first example of the purple gem of the same name. The ancient Greeks believed that for this reason, amethyst prevented drunkenness, and they and the Romans made wine cups out of the stone. Belief in the power of crystals such as this has persisted to the present day, with a modern boost in interest beginning with the counterculture of the 1960s and its exploration of alternative medicines and holistic beliefs. For many, semi-precious crystals are now more important than mere jewellery.

Some semi-precious stones are so lovely that they're mistaken for the much more expensive kind. The Imperial State Crown of the United Kingdom contains a famous red gem called the Black Prince's Ruby. It's been part of Britain's Crown Jewels since 1367, when it was given to Edward of Woodstock – known as the Black Prince for his heraldic crest – as payment for his aid in a civil war in Castile, Spain. At the time all red stones were referred to as rubies. It wasn't until after 1783 that advances in chemistry meant the Black Prince's Ruby could eventually be correctly identified. As well as the expected oxygen, aluminium and chromium, it also has magnesium in its crystalline makeup – making it not a precious ruby but a semi-precious spinel instead.

An ancient Sumerian statue of the goddess Inanna, made from translucent alabaster and with her eyes and navel (symbolic of life) detailed with vivid rose-pink rubies, the ancient world's most precious stone

SETTING COURSE WITH SUNSTONE

For centuries, legends have persisted that the Vikings used a special stone to help them track the position of the sun behind clouds, making their epic feats of navigation possible. Sunstone is a pretty, gold-flecked stone that would certainly have attracted their attention, but it's not capable of this. Iceland spar, however, is. A transparent calcite, it can polarise light, meaning you can hold it up to a cloudy sky and see a yellow dazzle when it's lined up with the sun.

Iceland spar might be the fabled Viking 'sólarsteinn' that the medieval seafarers used to navigate on their epic journeys, including from Greenland to Canada

The beguiling colours and shapes of crystals have captured our imagination for centuries and given rise to beliefs that they can soothe, heal, energise, and help us tap into deeper planes of being

How Crystals WORK

What can crystals do for us? Quite a lot, as it turns out...

You do crystal magic every day without even realising it. When you wake up and turn your phone alarm off, you touch a screen that has a Liquid Crystal Display (LCD). Your touch sends an electrical signal to the phone's interface that tells it to do something, whether that's turning your alarm off, checking your WhatsApp or opening TikTok. The liquid crystals in screens change colour when light is passed through them; by organising that light and the crystals it shines through, your phone shows you the app you want. The same technology powers your TV and the screens you see everywhere in everyday life. Or maybe you've printed something out recently? Inside each cartridge of printer ink there's a tiny crystal that responds to subsonic electrical vibrations called piezoelectrics. When you tell the printer to print, it sends an electrical pulse through those crystals and makes them vibrate, releasing a bubble of ink onto the paper. Crystals are also highly sensitive to radio frequencies and can pick them out of the air; in the early days of broadcasting a simple device made of crystal and metal inside a radio enabled you to listen to music over the airwaves. Silicon crystal semiconductors are at the heart of today's phones and computers, and scientists have experimented with using a type of fused quartz to store vast quantities of information and access it more quickly than current technology can. The power of crystals is all around you, in constant use.

Quartz is one of the most common and useful crystals. Made up of silicon and oxygen, it's the world's second-most common mineral (the first is feldspar, a group that contains beautiful crystals such as moonstone and labradorite). There are many different types of quartz to be found – amethyst, carnelian, agate, tiger's eye, aventurine and citrine are all quartzes. Like all crystals, their colour and properties are influenced by the elements in their crystalline makeup. As well as silicon and oxygen, citrine contains iron, which gives it its orange-yellow hue. Iron can also be responsible for amethyst's

GROW YOUR OWN

You can grow your own crystals in a cleaned-out jam jar using a relatively inexpensive kit, available from retailers including toy stores, science museums and Amazon. You won't be able to grow anything you can wear or use, but it's a fun experiment in seeing how crystals are formed!

You can grow single crystals in a jar, or 'crystal gardens' like these ones, using a simple kit you can buy online

Crystals captivate us with their beauty, but they're far more useful than mere adornment

"In the early days of broadcasting, a device made of crystal and metal inside a radio enabled you to listen to music over the airwaves"

purple and rose quartz's pink. Quartzes are used in clocks and watches. They have piezoelectric properties, so they often also turn up in printers. They can be custom-grown in a lab as well as found naturally. But they have more esoteric uses as well. Rose quartz is famous for its alleged healing and beautifying properties, making it a very common material for use in massage tools, particularly facial rollers and gua sha stones.

It's their sensitivity to intangible vibrations, combined with crystals' ability to receive, modulate, store and broadcast that makes proponents of crystals believe in their more arcane powers. Former scientist Rupert Sheldrake, now a parapsychology researcher and author, proposed a theory called 'morphic resonance' in which he stated his belief that natural systems – crystals among them – inherited and stored memories from others of their kind. One common example is growing successive crystal gardens in the same jar, and how they can follow the same pattern of growth as the previous layout, even when the jar has been sterilised and the starter chemicals are arranged differently. Sheldrake's theory was dismissed as pseudo-science and he was censured by the scientific community, and sceptics maintain that the only effect crystals produce in humans is a placebo – they only have an effect because we believe that they will. Many of the things that crystal proponents believe that crystals interact with – such as auras – are also considered pseudo-scientific, meaning there's little possibility of any definitive research proving (or disproving) those beliefs. Many of us, however, find we're drawn to particular kinds of crystals, or even repelled by others. Whether that's simply an aesthetic attraction or an affinity on a deeper vibrational level may never be definitively proven.

Types of CRYSTAL

Crystals come in all shapes and sizes, from their atomic structure to the way they are cut and carved, each crystal form unlocks a variety of properties and energies

When we discuss types of crystals, we could be talking about anything from their atomic structure or scientific category, to their most redeeming metaphysical qualities or the way they are cut and polished. For example, quartz crystals are a whole family of hard silica minerals with a tetrahedral molecular geometry. Known for their exceptional ability to calm and heal, quartz can be found in many forms from jewellery and polished points, to geodes and even lamps and bookends, and is available in various colours, offering it numerous guises including generic "rock crystal" amethyst, citrine, ametrine, herkimer diamond, agate, chalcedony, carnelian, onyx, jasper, prasiolite, aventurine and tiger's eye! Here, we delve into all the essential terminology you need to understand in order to get the very most out of your crystals, and to work out exactly which ones will work best for you!

NEED TO KNOW: TERMS

Not all crystals are in fact, well, crystals! While we may use the terms crystal, mineral and gemstone interchangeably, they each have a different, distinctive atomic structure

CRYSTALS Solids with an orderly, repeating pattern of atoms, ions and molecules.

MINERALS A naturally occurring inorganic substance (element or compound) that contains a crystalline structure within it at a microscopic level, ie a distinct uniform atomic composition and regularly repeating internal structure.

MINERALOID A mineral-like substance that occurs naturally (and often from organic origin), that does not have a crystalline structure, ie they have an organic or amorphous structure.

ROCKS A solid collection of minerals, generally two or more.

STONE A hard piece of mineral substance or rock.

GEMSTONE A piece of mineral crystal or mineraloid that is cut and polished and used in jewellery. There are precious stones (generally only diamonds, sapphires, rubies and emeralds) and semi-precious stones (all other gemstones, even if they are worth more money and rarer than a precious stone).

JEWEL A lustrous, cut and polished crystal used as an ornament or in jewellery. Jewel is used typically in reference to a precious stone, ie diamond, sapphire, ruby or emerald, but can refer to a semi-precious stone too.

Crystal Formation

All crystals, like everything in our world, are made up of atoms, but they don't all share the same atomic structure. Every crystal is formed thanks to these atoms arranging themselves in patterns, creating a distinctive lattice structure. The type of internal atomic lattice or molecular structure formed within the crystal defines which crystal system they belong to. Crystals belonging to the same system share the same lattice and therefore the same scientific properties, as well as many of the same metaphysical properties too! There are seven main crystal systems, each sharing a similar shaped lattice structure, as well as some with no lattice at all. By knowing the internal structure of each crystal, we can interpret their general external properties. The crystal systems are as follows:

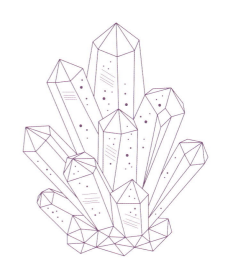

	STRUCTURE	EXAMPLES	PROPERTIES
	CUBIC (aka Isometric)	Diamond, pyrite, garnet, lapis lazuli, fluorite, sodalite, silver and gold	Grounding, cleansing and stabilising. Encourages creativity and structure.
	MONOCLINIC	Diopside, azurite, malachite, azulite, selenite, satin spar	Purifying, helpful for achieving physical balance and aiding perception.
	TRICLINIC	Turquoise, kyanite, labradorite, rainbow moonstone	Protection and encourages perception and intuition.
	TETRAGONAL	Rutile, apophyllite, zircon	Transformation, harmony and resolution. Encourages a balanced flow of energy.
	HEXAGONAL (includes trigonal sub-system)	Quartz, calcite, ruby, emerald, apatite, tourmaline	Aids organisation, balance and supportive energy.
	ORTHORHOMBIC	Topaz, peridot, chrysoberyl, tanzanite, iolite, aragonite, marcasite	Inspires energy and vibrancy. Cleanses, dispels and eases flow of information.
	AMORPHOUS OR ORGANIC	Amber, obsidian, shungite, jet, opal, moldavite, tektite, chrysocolla	Aids growth and release of toxic energy. Helpful for protection.

Crystal shapes

How a crystal is cut and polished (or not) can help to unlock its power

Crystals, minerals and stones are often available in a variety of shapes. Many crystals only reveal their true beauty after they have been cut and polished. Different processes, however, can change the potency of their properties. In many cases polishing crystals will make them tougher and more durable, while carving them into shapes can also enhance their healing potential. Polishing can also create a curved, smooth surface with no hard edges – which, according to feng shui, means energy flows more freely. Discover what each shape means here and you will be able to harness each crystal's true potential!

A CHIP OFF THE OLD BLOCK

When gemstones are used in jewellery they are prepared in one of two ways: cabochon or faceted. Cabochon is used most commonly for more opaque semi-precious stones and is achieved by simply shaping the stone and polishing it into one smooth and flat, often rounded form. It was the default way to prepare gemstones prior to the development of faceting. Faceted stones are cut with a flat top, many polished flat faces (called facets) across it and a pointed bottom in order to refract the light inside a translucent gem as well as on the outside. Faceting is a cutting technique commonly used for more translucent crystals, such as diamonds, rubies and sapphires, but it can also be used to make more opaque minerals sparkle. Engagement rings most often contain faceted gemstones in order to maximise their splendour. How a crystal is faceted determines the way in which its energy flows.

RAW
Potent power

BEST FOR LIVING SPACES, HEALING AND MAGIC

Raw specimens are crystals in their natural state with no cutting or polishing. They are very potent, radiating a strong, powerful energy. Some people may find their high vibrations overwhelming, so they are best kept in a large space and used for powerful magic and healing rituals.

FREEFORM
Gentle vibes

BEST FOR LIVING SPACES

These are rough specimens that are carved in order to reveal their beauty. Each one is unique and highly vibrational, but thanks to their carving, their energy is softer than their raw counterparts, making them ideal for displaying around your home.

POINTS
The amplifiers

BEST FOR MANIFESTATION, DIRECTING ENERGY

Towers or points are crystals with a point or face at the top and can be small or large with four or more sides. These points can occur naturally or can be carved and are useful for directing energy in crystal healing. There are a few other types of pointed crystals you may want to familiarise yourself with.

GENERATOR CRYSTALS
Crystal batteries

BEST FOR RECHARGING OTHER CRYSTALS

Generator crystals are towers with six equal sides meeting at a point. As they are a point, they are energy amplifiers, but thanks to their six-sided faces, they are particularly potent and often used for charging other crystals, like your own personal crystal battery.

CLUSTERS
Energy centres

BEST FOR MANIFESTATION, ENERGY CLEANSING, HEALING AND MEDITATION

Clusters are many naturally occurring points all joined together, making them incredibly powerful. They may be a mixture of crystal types, all unified by the adjoining base. They radiate energy outwards, purifying and cleansing everything around them.

GEODES
Diffusers

BEST FOR LIVING SPACES, CHARGING, AMPLIFYING AND SOFTENING THE ENERGY OF OTHER CRYSTALS

Geodes are cave-like hollow structures, often available in specialist stores or home decor suppliers. The most popular geodes are amethyst, citrine and other forms of quartz. They are great for charging and diffusing other smaller crystals – just pop them inside! Pieces of geodes, such as a chunk of small amethysts crystallised on a rock surface, are referred to as druzy crystals.

TUMBLE STONES
Portable power

BEST FOR EVERYDAY USE AND TRAVEL

Small, often rounded polished tumble stones are the easiest and cheapest way to incorporate crystals into your everyday life. They can be placed around your home and are small enough to keep in your pocket.

WANDS
Pressure point tools

BEST FOR MASSAGE AND HEALING

Wands are cut, polished and rounded at both ends, making them ideal for use on the body, as they direct the energy flow and are smooth enough to touch against the skin.

OTHER POPULAR SHAPES

PYRAMID Anchors and transmits intentions to the universe, an excellent manifestation tool.

SPHERE Emits radial energy and represents universal connection and cycles, perfect for divination!

EGG Represents fertility, new beginnings and stability.

CUBE Symbol of stability and grounding, excellent for meditation.

HEART Represents love and kindness, the perfect talisman for loved ones.

ANGEL A guardian angel that offers protection and connection to higher realms.

ANIMALS Represents the spirit of the chosen animal and brings with it the animal's associated energy.

MOONS Symbolic of the Moon itself, harnesses lunar energy and connects to cycles and emotions.

PALM/MEDITATION/WORRY STONES
Solace stones

BEST FOR MOMENTS OF ANXIETY, MEDITATION, GRIDDING

Palm stones are flat and smooth for stone to skin contact and energy transference. They are ideal for rubbing when you are feeling anxious or stressed and to use while practising mindfulness.

DOUBLE TERMINATED CRYSTALS
Transformational tools

BEST FOR HEALING, REIKI, CLEANSING, GRIDDING, MANIFESTATION

Double terminated crystals have points at both ends. They facilitate healing and magical work as their energy flows both ways. Negative energy enters at one end and is purified and transformed into positive energy to exit the other end. They are therefore excellent at removing stagnant energy and transferring and transmitting other crystals' energies in a grid.

How to choose
YOUR CRYSTALS

Where to find crystals and how to decide which ones to buy

Picking out crystals is first and foremost an instinctual task. The best way to select your crystals is to go to a specialist store devoted to rocks and minerals, jewellery or the esoteric. Another excellent place to source crystals is at museums – they often sell some wonderful specimens in their gift shops.

Next, just have a look at each crystal and notice what you are attracted to, what piece is drawing you to it? Take note what the crystal is and look it up – it's likely that the crystal is catching your eye because it has the properties that you are seeking. If you are lucky enough to stumble upon a dedicated crystals store, ask the staff to help you. They are guaranteed to have expertise and will know what they have in store that might interest you. They also may suggest crystals you might not have heard of before. Make sure you feel the crystals when you are choosing them. Pick them up and notice how they make you feel. If you are choosing one for somebody else, have them in your mind while you search.

If you can't get to a shop, there are numerous places online where you can source crystals, but be careful not to be caught out. Crystals are not cheap, and if the prices seem too good to be true, they probably are!

Where to buy

Crystals are cold to the touch, but so are synthetic replicas made from glass. Make sure you are sourcing your minerals from reputable sources, particularly when buying online. Here are some recommendations:
• Spirit Nectar (etsy.com/shop/thespiritnectar)
• The Psychic Tree (thepsychictree.co.uk)
• Crystal Vaults (crystalvaults.com)

• Sage Goddess (sagegoddess.com)
• Energy Muse (energymuse.com)
• Aquarian Soul (shopaquariansoul.com)
• Kacha Stones (kacha-stones.com)
• House of Intuition (houseofintuitionla.com)
• Moonrise Crystals (moonrisecrystals.com)
• Happy Soul (happysoulcrystals.com)
• Modern Mystic (modernmysticshop.com)

How to use your crystals

Once you've selected your crystals, what do you do with them? There are many ways in which you can use crystals to enrich your life and harness their energy. Their shapes and sizes all have their own benefits and specialities, as you can see from page 14. Tumble stones are perhaps one of the most versatile crystal forms as they are available in almost every crystal imaginable and can be kept in your pocket, your bra, inside a cage necklace or spiral (available in most specialist stores), in your car, beside your bed, to decorate your shelves, within the wax of a candle... you name it, they can go EVERYWHERE!

Another great option is jewellery. You can wear black grounding crystals around your neck as amulets of protection as they absorb negative energy and tap into your intuition with earrings of a crystal that corresponds to your third eye chakra (most purple-hued gems). Placing the correct crystal next to each of your chakras can work wonders for your health (see page 44), and finding the right spot within your home can help aid sleep (see page 70), shield you from harmful EMF and create a calming sanctuary (see page 75) or even work some serious magic (see page 104).

WHY NOT TRY?

If you are having trouble getting started with crystals, you can't go wrong by picking out your birthstone. For most, our monthly traditional birthstone is our first introduction into crystals. It's likely you were gifted your birthstone as a child, whether it was in the form of a tiny gem attached to a teddy bear, a simple chipped bracelet or, for the lucky ones, an heirloom ring. Here are the traditional and modern correspondences for each month:

BIRTH MONTH	TRADITIONAL BIRTHSTONE	MODERN BIRTHSTONE
January	Garnet	Garnet
February	Amethyst	Amethyst
March	Bloodstone	Aquamarine
April	Diamond	Diamond or quartz
May	Emerald	Emerald or chrysoprase
June	Pearl	Moonstone
July	Ruby	Carnelian
August	Sardonyx (onyx)	Peridot
September	Sapphire	Sapphire
October	Opal	Tourmaline
November	Topaz	Golden topaz or citrine
December	Turquoise or lapis lazuli	Blue topaz or tanzanite

"Placing the correct crystal next to your chakras can work wonders for your health"

19

How to care
FOR YOUR CRYSTALS

To get the best results from your crystals, you will need to cleanse and charge them!

Crystals can be delicate, so knowing how to care for them properly is important. Some crystals are damaged by water, while others can be brittle and easily chipped and scratched. It is important to bear this in mind when you are cleansing and charging your crystals in order to make use of their energy and powers.

Before we use crystals for healing or magical means, we must first do a cleanse to rid any negative or stagnant energies from them. It is also wise to cleanse any new jewellery you buy before you wear it, and even after a particularly stressful day!

There are numerous ways in which you can

WAYS TO CLEANSE YOUR CRYSTALS

Smoke or incense

Smudging with a simple stick of incense or a stick made of dried, bound herbs, can be used to restore your crystals' natural frequency. Simply light the incense and waft it all around the crystal.

Selenite

A flat piece of selenite can be used to cleanse your crystals thanks to its powerfully potent purifying and cleansing energy. Simply place the crystals on top of the selenite for a few hours and let the crystal work its magic.

Water

Running water is perfect for cleansing and cleaning almost anything, including crystals. Just be careful not to use this method on any water-soluble crystals – check for the icon beside the crystals throughout this book to check if a crystal can be cleansed this way. Celestite and selenite are two crystals that are never to be cleansed with water, and advised to be kept out of wet spaces!

Salt

A salt water bath or burying your crystals in salt can be great techniques for cleansing hardier crystals. Use Himalayan salt between healing treatments, or simply put your crystals beside a salt lamp. We don't recommend this technique for delicate crystals or as an everyday cleansing technique.

Breathwork

Meditative breathing combined with your intention to cleanse and recharge your crystal can foster and strengthen the bond between you and your crystals. All you need to do is visualise your crystal letting go of the negative energy and being filled up with pure energy and let out a strong cleansing breath, literally blowing away the debris.

cleanse your crystals, with some better suited to certain crystals than others. Selenite, for example, cannot be cleansed with water (and in fact, shouldn't need cleansing at all!), while varieties of quartz are perfectly safe to use running water on.

It is essential to ensure you remove any dust and debris from your crystals, especially if you have them on display in your home. A layer of fine dust reduces the electrostatic charge your crystal emits, so it's important to get rid of it. Water is the ultimate tool for this, but for the more delicate gems, simply polish with a dry cloth or soft brush (such as a makeup brush) and always avoid any harsh chemicals – these can damage their surface and even affect their energy.

Cleansing your crystals also helps establish a connection between you and your crystals, helping to open up a clear-flowing bond between your own energy and the healing magic of your crystals.

Once you have cleansed your crystals, you may want to charge them. Charging crystals is essential to ensure they remain activated. When it comes to spellwork, programming crystals is vital in order to achieve the outcome you require. Crystal programming establishes your intention for the crystal and requires you to speak to the crystal directly – simply tell the crystal what you desire from it. Outside of spellwork, you don't need to program a crystal, but it can be a very useful technique if you find that you want to manifest something in particular, such as healing.

Get in the habit of looking after your crystals to ensure optimum energy output

WAYS TO CHARGE YOUR CRYSTALS

Sunlight
The sun is a strong, energetic force that will remove stale energies and reinvigorate your crystals. Place your crystals out in the sun or along a window sill where the sun pours in for a few hours. Don't leave crystals in a sunny spot though – many darker coloured crystals will fade if they are left in the sun too long!

Moonlight
Moonlight is a potent yet gentle cleansing and rejuvenating energy and, unlike the sun, is safe for all crystals. Simply lay out your crystals on the window sill under the full or new moon for supercharged crystals.

Earth
"Earthing" or "grounding" your crystals is a traditional method used by divination practitioners. Bury your crystals in some soil, such as a house plant or a flower bed (don't forget to mark where you put them!), and leave overnight. Don't use this method for delicate clusters or metallic crystals as they may rust.

Music
A sound bath will harmonise your crystals with the vibrational waves of music. Strum a guitar, chant or sing your mantra and intention or use a singing bowl or bell.

Visualisation
Power up your crystal by simply meditating on your crystal and visualising a light filling it.

Crystal GRIDDING

Learn how to bring a new depth to your relationship with crystals by combining their energy with powerful sacred geometry in the form of crystal grids

There are few more powerful ways to release crystal energy than using sacred geometry. Whether you want to bring your crystals into play in matters of love, health, finance or wellbeing, a crystal grid could take you to a whole other level of understanding.

A crystal grid is an arrangement of stones that is laid out in a very deliberate pattern with the intention to create a positive outcome. By choosing a complementary group of stones and setting them out in a sacred configuration, you'll direct the flow of energies for your own specific intention. It's a wonderful way to harness and amplify the deepest power of crystals.

Crystal grids can provide a great passive energy in any space, but you can use them in manifesting and healing rituals, as they enable the crystals' energies to really flow towards the desired purpose. Directing this energy can create a powerful source of protection and you can use that flow to harness your own powers too, by employing crystal grids in meditation or divination. Though the concept of sacred geometry might sound a little daunting, it's really just a matter of following your own intuition and letting the crystals guide you towards the right path.

Whether you want to incorporate them into other rituals or keep them simple, there is a crystal grid for every occasion and intention and your intuition will tell you which is right for you. Whether it's the infinity of circles or spiral patterns such as the triskelion, with

their intricate and twisting focus, or the protection of five-pointed stars, there is a huge range of options.

Whatever you choose, designing and working with crystal grids doesn't have to be a solo activity. The crystals will respond to your energy and those of whoever is involved in the creation of the grids. If you have a group of crystal-loving friends, creating grids together will be a wonderful way to set positive intentions and manifest the outcomes you truly desire.

NUMEROLOGY

Numerology and crystal gridding have a naturally empowering relationship and by choosing a certain number of crystals, you can really harness their power and potential. You can set a more focused intention by working with the numerological qualities of different crystals too, to bring even more meaning and strength to the grids you make. Here are some key numerology numbers and their meanings:

2 – Balance and harmony
3 – Creativity and hidden skills
5 – Dynamism and strength
7 – Truth and intuition

INFINITY

The lemniscate symbolises infinity. Arrange your crystals into this shape if you feel as though things are out of balance and are looking for some cleansing, rebalancing energy. This neverending figure of eight symbolises opposites of all sorts, from male and female to darkness and light, and it reminds us that every ending is really just another beginning. It's a great option if there are two separate or conflicting elements that need to be drawn together with the intention of moving forwards. Because the pattern has no ending, the energy is in a constant state of flow, bringing in positivity and pushing out negativity.

The neverending infinity symbol reminds us that every end is a new beginning

Types of Grid

Crystal grids come in a variety of designs and which sacred geometric arrangement you choose will depend on how you want to focus their energies. You can draw your own or download printable templates online, or even buy grid patterns as printed cloth mats or wooden templates. You could even create a star or sun grid with a focus stone that won't need a template at all.

CIRCLE

Our ancestors knew when they constructed ancient stone circles that the never-ending circle has a power all its own. This is the perfect choice if you're looking for strength and protection in any space.

TRIANGLE

The triangle brings in positive energy and neutralises the negative, creating a safe space wherever you place it, not only inside the shape but outside of its edges too. Triangle grids make an excellent choice for healing conflict and disharmony.

SQUARE

This simple and basic grid is a great place to start with your crystal gridding. A square grid offers protection while anchoring your intention in its solid, symmetrical shape. You might use this grid to provide clarity or calm a troubled space. It's also a great option for containing and calming negative energies.

METATRON'S CUBE

If you find yourself struggling with self-criticism and struggle to really see the good around you, working with Metatron's Cube might provide the focus you need. Choosing this grid will help you focus your intention of bringing out positive thoughts to manifest happiness and positivity.

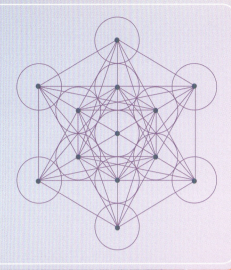

FLOWER OF LIFE

Sometimes self-esteem and confidence can be a struggle, but the Flower of Life will focus crystal energy to build the best you you can be. Just as a flower blooms from a simple seed, this grid will help your inner self blossom.

SEED OF LIFE

If you're looking for something that will really focus your creative energies and help you see a project through to its end, this is the grid for you. It will strengthen good work habits and manifest whatever goals you nurture, helping you to reach your full potential.

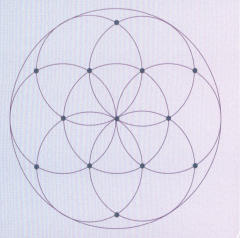

How to Create a Crystal Grid

Creating your own crystal grid will take your practice with crystals to a new level and open up a world of possibilities. Whether you're working with printed, wooden or hand-drawn templates, setting up your own crystal grid is as simple as it is rewarding.

1 Set your intention

The very first step in building a crystal grid is also the most important. When you think about which grid to use and which crystals you'll place in it, it's vital that you've set your intention so your grid can manifest your dreams, whatever they might be. So take some time to create a pleasing space, bringing in whatever elements you need whether that's the right music or symbols, maybe some candles and personal talismans.

2 Choose your grid

When it comes to choosing your grid, there are two great methods to use. The first is to look into the purpose of each grid and choose the one that suits your intention best or which might work best with a favourite crystal. Alternatively, browse through the grids and plump for the one your intuition draws you to. Then you can download or draw whichever pattern template best suits your goal.

3 Choose your focus stone

Each grid needs a large focus stone, which sits at its heart and is used to focus the energies and powers of the crystals that make up the pattern. Always choose a focus stone that represents your intention for the grid, to ensure that you're making it as powerful as possible. The large central stone will channel and focus the power of the grid so if you aren't sure what to use, clear quartz is a reliable standby.

4 Choose your smaller stones

Way stones and desire stones are the smaller crystals that will populate the grid. Way stones are arranged in the spaces around the focus stones and you should choose them according to how you'll reach your goal. Focus on your journey and choose the stones that answer. The desire stones on the outer grid should align closely with your ultimate desire. As you choose them, think really closely about what you desire and listen to your instincts when you make your choices.

5 Set up and activate your grid

Once you've placed your stones and grid, activate it by clearly stating your intention as you focus on the stone at the centre of the grid and imagine a light radiating out into the other crystals, bathing the grid in warmth. If it helps, you can use whatever words and gestures feel right to build your own activation ritual. You could even use an activator wand such as a quartz point, touching each stone as you repeat your intention.

6 What next?

Be sure to check in on your grid now and then to restate your intention and cleanse your crystals from time to time, but not too often. When your grid has achieved its purpose, dismantle it by taking each crystal in turn and thanking it for its work. Then sit them out in the sunlight or moonlight for a few hours to let them recharge their energies ready for another day, while you cleanse the space with smoke.

"Always choose a focus stone that represents your intention for the grid, to ensure that you're making it as powerful as possible"

Essential Crystals
FOR YOUR COLLECTION

These crystals are the ideal tools for those starting out on their journey into a world of natural healing

BEST FOR
Clarity, balance, communication, healing of body, mind and soul, inner peace and healing, spiritual awareness

ELEMENT
Water

CHAKRA
Crown & Third Eye

ASSOCIATED STAR SIGNS
Pisces, Aquarius, Capricorn, Virgo & Sagittarius

APPEARANCE
Deep purple, violet

SHAPES & FORMS
Cubes, pyramids, spheres, tumbled shapes, rough chunks, crystal points

AVAILABILITY
Common

Amethyst

This luminous stone has been celebrated since 25,000 BCE, with the Romans, Greeks and even the ancient Egyptians all drawn by the healing powers of this protective purple crystal. Its very name translates from the Greek word 'améthystos', meaning 'not intoxicated', and it promotes sobriety, clear thinking and tranquillity.

Amethyst acts as a natural tranquilliser helping to balance fears, moods, anger and anxiety and alleviate grief and sadness. It holds strong healing powers and guards against negative energies such as ill wishes from others, electromagnetic stress and various forms of geopathic stress from the Earth's negative energy vibrations. This powerhouse of a stone opens up intuition and spiritual awareness, activating psychic abilities.

Amethyst is hugely beneficial for relieving insomnia, as well as understanding and remembering dreams. Because it has such a powerfully calming effect, it not only helps to stimulate the mind but also the body by improving motivation and assists in enhancing memory.

An incredible healer, this crystal strengthens the immune system, relieves psychological stress and pain, releases tension and eases headaches, all in addition to boosting the production of hormones and cleansing the blood. It even helps to fine-tune both the metabolism and endocrine system.

"Amethyst is a natural tranquilliser, helping to balance fears, moods, anger and anxiety"

Amethyst is connected with the Greek god of wine, Dionysus; the stone was originally used to cure hangovers

Orange calcite

This vibrant orange stone is one of creativity and filled with powerful cleansing energies. It is associated with higher consciousness and is a planetary stone of the Moon, Sun and the planet Venus. It was favoured by the ancient Egyptians as an earth element for cleansing energy to remove emotional and physical blockages and negative vibrations. This rock-forming mineral is found in igneous, metamorphic and sedimentary rocks and helps to facilitate meditation, as well as assist in spiritual growth, expanding your awareness and connecting you to the realms of higher consciousness. Often used in trance and out-of-body work, it gives you the ability to self-heal and repair, strengthen and restore both your mind and body, and stimulate a positive flow of energy. It resonates with the solar plexus and base chakras, particularly the sacral chakra, and has great cleaning abilities, clearing our energy centres, connecting us to the planet.

Orange calcite balances emotions and releases feelings of fear and anxiety by dispelling blocked and negative energies from your aura and eliminating pollutants. It also amplifies your energy and fills you with optimism, empowering you to come to terms with all of life's chapters, let go of regret and guilt and embrace fresh inspiration. On top of all this, it boosts emotional intelligence, vitality, and kidney and liver function, plus it assists in unlocking erotic energies.

BEST FOR
Growth, development, happiness, hope, unlocks energies

·

ELEMENT
Fire

CHAKRA
Sacral & Root

ASSOCIATED STAR SIGNS
Cancer

·

APPEARANCE
A crystalline texture in a rich orange, amber or honey-yellow

·

SHAPES & FORMS
Jewellery, figurines, pyramids, rough and tumbled stones and talismans

·

AVAILABILITY
Common

As one of the most versatile healing crystals, orange calcite has numerous spiritual qualities

"This rock-forming mineral helps to facilitate meditation, as well as assist in spiritual growth"

"It evokes feelings of inner peace and deep healing and is often used in times of sadness and grief"

Stone masks made from rose quartz have been recovered from both Roman and Egyptian tombs, ensuring beauty and calm in the afterlife

BEST FOR
Unconditional love, kindness, friendship, self-love, caring, romantic love

ELEMENT
Earth & Water

CHAKRA
Heart

ASSOCIATED STAR SIGNS
Taurus & Libra

APPEARANCE
Light pink, rose

SHAPES & FORMS
Tumbled, various shapes, jewellery, beauty products, talismans, raw cluster, sphere

AVAILABILITY
Common

Rose quartz

This pale pink quartz is the stone of universal love. From platonic to motherly love, it covers all bases and opens the heart, encouraging unconditional love to flow all around. This crystal of love and energy comes under the spiritual power centre the Temple of Light, making it a favourite among healers. This quartz makes a popular talisman or charm, its colour representing calmness, love and compassion. Rose quartz also assists in self-love and encourages self-worth, acceptance and self-forgiveness and protects against outside negativities and pollutants. It evokes feelings of inner peace and deep healing and is often used for comfort in times of sadness and grief. This quartz has amazing healing powers, helping to hasten recovery from illness, strengthen the heart, reduce high blood pressure, heal kidney issues and improve chest and lung problems. It can even alleviate vertigo and is often used to increase fertility and protect women during pregnancy. Belonging to the 'Great Mother' stones, this quartz links your heart to the Earth, and while you are sleeping it blocks out nightmares and only allows happy, restful dreams to filter into your subconscious.

Clear quartz

Known as the 'Master Healer', clear quartz is a fantastic starting stone for your crystal healing journey. With The Great Mother as its deity and in alignment with the Sun and Moon, this crystal is a hub of protective and receptive energy. Clear quartz takes and absorbs energy, clearing it of negativity, storing it and releasing it, helping to balance the body on all levels (planes): spiritual, emotional, physical and mental. It has a hugely enlightening effect on the body's chakras, particularly in balancing the crown chakra, helping promote relaxation and bringing in purified energy.

Often referred to as the 'stone of the mind', clear quartz unlocks memory and focuses the mind, enhancing concentration and learning capacity in addition to bringing the body back into balance. This stone of harmony awakens your intuition, helping to clarify your emotions and thought process.

Clear quartz oscillates at the very highest vibration of all crystals, the stone resembling perpetually frozen water, the clearness symbolising clarity of vision, the white and open heart. It can be used to charge all other crystals and is fantastic when used for communicating with spirits; it is often used to counter black magic.

"Clear quartz unlocks memory and focuses the mind"

Clear quartz contains pure silicon, which can be used to make numerous computer components

BEST FOR
Power, protection, diagnostic healing, psychic abilities, energy, clarity, calmness, harmony

ELEMENT
Fire, Water, Air & Earth

CHAKRA
Crown

ASSOCIATED STAR SIGNS
Leo & Aries

APPEARANCE
Colourless and translucent through to cloudy and milky

SHAPES & FORMS
Cubes, spheres, pyramids, tumbled, crystal points, rough chunks, clusters, animals, hearts

AVAILABILITY
Common

Tiger's eye

As the name suggests, tiger's eye is a stone of powerful protection and is a crystal of the Sun. Particularly good for assisting in colour healing and used in treating both mind and body, it may even bring you good luck. It assists in promoting mental clarity and is often used when treating psychosomatic issues, helps to ease anxiety and dispel fear. Tiger's eye releases tensions and rebalances the body, imbuing it with positive energy, courage and purpose. It will come as no surprise that this crystal is used when treating optical and eye issues as well as throat and reproductive problems. Tiger's eye can strengthen bones, alleviate pain and help the body to release toxins.

Both red and blue tigers' eyes boast these attributes, and in addition blue exudes calmness, particularly beneficial for sufferers of intense anxiety, phobias and stress. Red tiger's eye, on the other hand, has the opposite effect. With the fire element in its chakra, it can spark a low sex drive or slow metabolism into life.

"Tiger's eye releases tensions and rebalances the body"

BEST FOR
Power, courage, integrity, clear thinking, protection, grounding, balances the soul

ELEMENT
Fire & Earth

CHAKRA
Sacral & Solar Plexus

ASSOCIATED STAR SIGNS
Capricorn

APPEARANCE
Golden-brown, blue, red

SHAPES & FORMS
Cabochon, carved, finished as ovals, rounds, pears and freeform shape

AVAILABILITY
Common

Used traditionally to ward off curses, tiger's eye was once considered to be more precious than gold

" It can help to treat depression and neuralgia and dispels resentment and envy"

The ancient Egyptians believed its red hues represented male energy and the orange colour female energy and referred to it as 'the setting sun'

BEST FOR
Individuality, courage, past life recall, memory, self-esteem

·

ELEMENT
Fire

CHAKRA
Sacral & Root

ASSOCIATED STAR SIGNS
Virgo, Leo, Taurus & Cancer

·

APPEARANCE
Almost black, pink, pale orange

·

SHAPES & FORMS
Rough stones, pyramids, tumbled stones, pointed crystals, wands

·

AVAILABILITY
Common

Carnelian

Named by the ancient Egyptians as the sunset stone, carnelian is a symbol of wisdom and wealth. This unique stone stimulates creativity, enhancing a person's motivation for success and making decisions. A stability stone, carnelian sharpens concentration and restores vitality. It helps to banish any negative conditioning and is particularly helpful for overcoming various kinds of abuse by removing emotional negativity. It can help to treat depression and neuralgia and dispels resentment and envy, instead bringing positivity by removing anger and negative thoughts and moods. Carnelian also helps in assisting the absorption of vitamins and minerals, accelerates healing, ensures good blood supply around the body and boosts fertility.

This powerful stone is ideal for healing as it is believed to stimulate the body's own healing processes, enabling it to reset into a balanced state. It is also beneficial for healing the lungs, liver, blood, skin conditions and spleen and acts as a defence against negative energies.

> "Jade helps us to build strong emotional support systems, reminds us to love"

Jade can be carved into various shapes and is a popular material for gua sha and facial massage rollers thanks to its purifying properties

BEST FOR
Good luck, abundance, peace, prosperity, love, strength, purification, harmony

·

ELEMENT
Earth

CHAKRA
Heart

ASSOCIATED STAR SIGNS
Virgo & Gemini

·

APPEARANCE
Translucent green

·

SHAPES & FORMS
Wands, shapes, tumbled stones, spheres, hearts

·

AVAILABILITY
Common

Jade

A gem that is often associated with China, green jade attracts abundance and good luck. In the Far East, it was often used as a symbol of greatness, grandeur and leadership. Also known as Imperial jade or Nephrite jade, green jade's soothing, calm energy encourages positivity, peace and joy, in addition to attracting true, loyal relationships. Associated with the heart chakra thanks to its distinctive green hue, jade helps us to build strong emotional support systems, reminds us to love and be loved, and also to nurture who and what is important to us. It can also aid us in healing from dysfunctional families or toxic past relationships.

Green jade is also a stone of inspiration, and emboldens us to put our ideas into action. It encourages tolerance, inspires hope and assists logical thinking and problem solving. Keep jade as a talisman to aid with autoimmune disorders and chronic stress. It is an excellent filter stone – it will help you to filter out toxic energies and remove yourself from problematic relationships. It also works on a physical level, aiding with adrenal glands, metabolism, and all elimination systems, including the lymphatic, digestive and urinary systems (particularly kidney health). Thanks to its associations with luck, it's also the perfect charm for anyone trying for a baby.

Obsidian

Originating from volcanic glass, obsidian is a protective stone that enhances truth and shields against negativity by absorbing negative environmental energies and preventing psychic interference. This crystal helps to stimulate growth by drawing out tension from the body and alleviating mental stresses, clearing the mind of confusion and bringing clarity. It urges you to question who you are, your purpose and encourages you to explore new horizons. It also promotes strength and compassion by removing traumas and emotional blockages to clear a path to fulfilment.

Specific colours of obsidian have additional attributes. Snowflake obsidian, for example, provides great balance for the mind, body and spirit, and as a stone of purity it also assists with loneliness and inner centring. Its black counterpart dissolves negative energies, repels intrusive thoughts and increases self-control. For many centuries this black shiny stone has been a way to connect the physical to the spiritual world, making it hugely popular in many cultures across the globe for its heightened metaphysical properties.

"Specific colours of obsidian have additional attributes"

BEST FOR
Transformation, psychic ability, purification, fulfilment

·

ELEMENT
Earth & Fire

CHAKRA
Root

ASSOCIATED STAR SIGNS
Scorpio & Sagittarius

·

APPEARANCE
Black, brown, silvery

·

SHAPES & FORMS
Cubes, pyramids, spheres, tumbled, hearts, rough chunks, animals, pyramids

·

AVAILABILITY
Common

Arrowheads and other artefacts made from obsidian have been discovered on archeological digs in the Saguaro National Park in Arizona, US

*Due to its density, hematite can block X-rays
and it is often used to protect against radiation*

Hematite

Hematite is the mineral form of iron oxide and a grounding stone that protects the mind, body and soul. Hematite promotes feelings of security, fills the soul with strength and stiffens willpower. This steely stone of the mind assists in improved concentration and helps to treat both insomnia and anxiety. Hematite also prevents the absorption of negativity, particularly that of other people and outside influences, and also dissipates any that you yourself might be experiencing. It creates a balanced equilibrium between the body's physical and ethereal nervous systems, focusing positive emotions and energy.

Offering a range of benefits, hematite stimulates blood supply, assists in the formation of red blood cells, supports the kidneys, and heals fractures and spinal alignment. It can even help to combat addictions such as smoking and overeating.

By revitalising tissue and lifting blood circulation, this traditional remedy can diminish the impact of a headache, massaging away the pain while keeping you grounded and calm. Known for its ability to protect, this silver-coloured iron oxide compound can reduce blood clotting and has been used to stem excessive bleeding, which explains why warriors and expectant mothers have kept a piece close at hand throughout history.

> *"It creates a balanced equilibrium between the body's physical and ethereal nervous systems"*

BEST FOR
Protection, focus, courage, optimism, trust, stability

·

ELEMENT
Fire & Earth

CHAKRA
Root

ASSOCIATED STAR SIGNS
Aries & Aquarius

·

APPEARANCE
Black, silvery-grey, steel, red, brown

·

SHAPES & FORMS
Raw crystal, tumbles, polished, jewellery

·

AVAILABILITY
Common

Amazonite

Sometimes known as Amazon stone, amazonite is a soothing crystal and a green variety of the feldspar mineral. Its name is a tribute to the mythical warrior-women said to have inhabited the Amazon and lived on their terms. The energy of this stone fittingly evokes personal truth and immense courage.

One of its more impressive features is that it helps in manifesting self and universal love, encouraging you to acknowledge different points of view and understand both sides. It calms the nervous system and brain, helping to alleviate fear and worry and dispel any emotional traumas, thereby balancing energies and keeping health at an optimum level. It removes negative energies, absorbs microwaves and protects against electromagnetic pollution too. It is also useful for sufferers of osteoporosis and relieves painful muscle spasms. Due to Amazonite being a potassium feldspar stone, it cannot be left in water for any length of time, and once it has had contact with water, it renders it undrinkable and dangerous to your health.

BEST FOR
Psychic vision, prophecy, clairvoyance, integrity, inspires truth

·

ELEMENT
Water & Earth

CHAKRA
Heart & Throat

ASSOCIATED STAR SIGNS
Virgo

·

APPEARANCE
Semi-opaque blue-green with cream swirls

·

SHAPES & FORMS
Animals, hearts, tumbled, cubes, spheres, rough chunks

·

AVAILABILITY
Common

Amazonite can balance the feminine and masculine energies in the body

"It calms the nervous system and brain, helping to alleviate fear and worry"

37

Health

40
Introduction to
crystal healing

·

44
Chakras

·

48
How to heal
with crystals

·

52
Crystals for your health

Introduction to crystal
HEALING

Discover how the use of crystal healing
has grown over the centuries, how to practise
it and the impact it has on body and soul

Healing crystals are believed to work on the premise that they affect the individual in two ways: through vibration, where the crystals alter the vibration of the body's molecules to match the vibrational energy of that particular crystal; and via the mindset, in which the crystals harness the power of the mind, providing a source of inspiration and creativity.

The history of crystals being used for the purpose of healing stretches back thousands of years, and has taken place all over the world. For instance, in India, they were used as part of a holistic form of treatment known as Ayurveda. Dating back to more than 5,000 years ago, the word translates from Sanskrit as 'science of life', and utilised crystals as a means to channel positive and healing energy flow into the body, drawing negative energy out in the process.

Dating back to a similar length of time, healing crystals were also used in Chinese medicine. Jade was particularly highly valued as a kidney healing stone, as it was in South America and later New Zealand. Other civilisations to prominently involve healing crystals in everyday society were the Sumerians, who included crystals in their magic formulas; the Egyptians, who utilised them for the purposes of protection and health; and the Greeks, who among other things, wore amethyst to treat drunkenness and hangovers!

To this day, Native Americans also continue to use medicine wheels. Made from an arranged collection of different crystals, it is intended as a compass of energies to be used when guidance is needed. Seen as an intrinsic part of their spirituality, they represent their connection to Earth and the sky.

Healing crystals continued to pop up throughout history. Their use was accepted in Renaissance times, and there is a record in the 13th century of someone being accused of stealing a gem from Henry III that was believed to make the wearer invincible. They fell from favour during the Age of Enlightenment, but began to be used again during the 19th century. By the 1980s, their use increased further thanks to New Age culture, with various old traditions being incorporated into numerous healing methods.

Today, practitioners of crystal healing incorporate the various methods and lessons learned through history. Here is a look at some of the most notable ways in which crystal healing is put into action.

> "The history of crystals being used for healing stretches back thousands of years"

DID YOU KNOW?

Clear quartz (sometimes simply called rock crystal), is also known as "The Master Healer". If you are keen to harness the power of crystals for healing, clear quartz is the essential crystal to have on hand. It will also amplify the healing energies of any other crystals you are using.

Jewellery

To benefit the most from the vibrational energy of crystals, it makes sense to have them in close proximity. Although they can be placed on people when they are lying down, incorporating them as part of an outfit is more practical on a day-to-day basis.

Meditation

An effective means of grounding and centring yourself, holding or focusing on a crystal can help you to return to meditation if your thoughts start to wander.

Decoration

If wearing them isn't an option, it's easy enough to place crystals around the home. Being in close proximity to crystals means they can be benefited from both vibrationally and from a mindset perspective.

Massage

Crystals have even been incorporated into a number of different types of holistic treatments, such as facials and massages. By adding crystals to a massage, a therapist can raise the level of wellness by three primary actions: clearing, energising and balancing. As well as reducing blocked energy in the mind and soul, they can be used to reduce muscle pain and tension both vibrationally and physically.

Polished crystals can be utilised as tools in massage treatments. Palm stones can be placed upon a client's palms in a similar fashion to a hot stone massage, while wands and tumbled stones can be used to access pressure points for acupressure and aid with deep tissue work and lymphatic drainage.

Crystals also work vibrationally and suitable crystals can simply be placed near or on the client within a treatment room, along with aromatherapy and plants to create a relaxing environment. The crystals have the ability to remove negativity and harmful toxins from the environment, encourage stress relief, harmonise emotions, energise and restore the soul, and bring the body and energy field back into balance. This energy field is often referred to as someone's aura, and rebalancing and centring it has often proved to be a focal point of healing crystals' intended use.

"Polished crystals can be utilised as tools in massage treatments"

"Crystals can be carried around with you to benefit from their positive energy"

Reiki

Coming from the Japanese words 'rei' and 'ki', meaning 'universal' and 'life energy' respectively, this involves placing the palms of the hand lightly on the body for a period of time (hence why it is sometimes referred to as 'palm healing'). It is intended to help the flow of energy around the body, in the process reducing stress, relieving pain and increasing healing. Crystals can be utilised to facilitate this energy flow.

Chromotherapy

Also referred to as 'colour therapy', chromotherapy uses the visible spectrum to heal the physical, mental and spiritual energy balances thought to lead to disease. To assist with this, crystals can be carried around with you to benefit from their positive energy. The benefits will depend on the colour of the crystals.

Sound therapy

One of the more innovative ways in which crystals have been used for healing purposes is via sound therapy. Crystals each have a frequency that can be heard in certain circumstances – to achieve this, place them in a bowl, and stay attuned. The effects of this can be manifest, potentially healing a number of physical, emotional and spiritual maladies.

With a huge variety of crystals that can be used for healing purposes and numerous ways to put them into use, there is undoubtedly a demand and a market for healing crystals.

AURAS, AND HOW TO HEAL THEM

Crystals can be used to heal the aura. Areas that need to be repaired are often known as 'auric tears', which are susceptible to the infiltration of negative energy. Crystals to use for the purpose of healing auras include:

Celestite
for purifying auras and refreshing your mood

Amethyst
for rejuvenating the body and mind

Kunzite
for aligning the body with spirituality

Selenite
for drawing out negative energy

Lepidolite
for strengthening the aura in advance of relationships

A strong aura is important, denoting people who are kind, compassionate and supportive to others, so maintaining one in this way can go a long way towards ensuring happiness.

43

Chakras
THE ESSENTIAL GUIDE

Everything you need to know about the body's energy centres and what to do when they become disconnected

When talking about crystal healing, chakras are often mentioned. Their significance can't be understated, as they are what enable the crystals to have the effect they do.

First written about over 4,000 years ago in ancient India, chakras are energy centres located within certain areas of the body that serve as connecting points between its thousands of energy channels. They draw in and expend energy, helping you to feel healthy and function properly. There are seven main chakras within the body: the crown; brow; throat; heart; solar plexus; sacral and base of spine.

Each crystal is closely associated with a particular chakra – placing it on, or as close to the relevant chakra as possible, will help the body to clean and energise this area. This technique is known as 'laying of stones'. In this feature, we will go into more detail about the various chakras and the different functions that they serve.

Is your chakra out of balance?

When one of your chakras is blocked or out of balance, you may feel unbalanced and disconnected yourself. You can check your chakras by using a crystal pendulum. This works by amplifying the energy produced by each chakra.

First, lie down on your back, and have a friend hold the pendulum a few inches above your body at the site of each chakra, writing down the direction and size of the swing for each location. Then roll over and have them do the same thing. The results have different meanings:

- **Clockwise** The chakra is open, energy is in balance and flowing freely.
- **Counterclockwise** The chakra is closed, energy is restricted and out of balance.
- **A straight line** The chakra is partially open or closed, signifying an energy imbalance and/or partial blockage.
- **Elliptical swinging** An imbalance on either side, meaning that while energy is flowing, it's unbalanced on one or both sides and could be overactive.
- **No movement** The chakra is completely blocked, no energy is flowing through.

ROOT
Muladhara

Four Petal Lotus

LOCATION
Base of the spine

ELEMENT
Earth

CRYSTALS
Ruby, hematite, red jasper, garnet, smoky quartz, black tourmaline, obsidian

KEY WORDS
Balance, stability, grounding, security, energy

ASSOCIATED PHYSIOLOGY:
Sexual development & function, sex hormones, legs & lower body, pelvis

BALANCED:
Anchored and grounded in reality. Self-confident and focused, organised and action-driven, full of energy, fit and active.

UNBALANCED:
Difficulty sleeping, bowel issues, incontinence, weight gain and loss, fatigue, weakened immunity, leg, foot and hip pain, pelvic pain, lower back issues. Aggressive, angry or irritable. Anxiety and depression. Disorganised, disconnected, and lacking in focus. Low self-esteem and confidence. Stress and feeling trapped.

HOW TO ALIGN
Try simple yoga poses that activate the legs. Earth or ground yourself with crystals or by physically feeling the ground between your toes. Fill your home with nature – get hold of some plants and rocks! Eat healthy. Walk, run, hike in nature. Try some gardening.

SACRAL
Svadhishthana

Six Petal Lotus

LOCATION
Below the navel

ELEMENT
Water

CRYSTALS
Carnelian, orange calcite,
peach moonstone, amber, citrine

KEY WORDS
Sexuality, sensuality, creativity,
emotion, fantasy, feminine energy

ASSOCIATED PHYSIOLOGY:
Kidney, bladder, reproductive organs
& genitals

BALANCED:
Constantly have new ideas, in tune
with your own desire and pleasures,
fluidity of expression, particularly in regards
to wants and needs in relationships.

UNBALANCED:
Anaemia, lower back pain, spleen and
kidney issues, joint problems,
hypoglycaemia, water retention,
menstruation problems, erectile dysfunction
and reproductive health issues.
Conflict, thriving on drama and experiencing
unhealthy relationships. Lacking creativity,
fatigue, insecure, detached and have a low
or unusually high libido.

HOW TO ALIGN
Eat a range of orange foods. Stretch your
hips. Tap into your creativity by trying
writing, drawing, acting, photography,
sculpture, dance or anything that gets
those juices flowing.

SOLAR PLEXUS
Manipura

Ten Petal Lotus

LOCATION
Upper abdomen

ELEMENT
Fire

CRYSTALS
Yellow calcite, lemon quartz,
pyrite, tiger's eye

KEY WORDS
Ambition, power, confidence,
personality, intellect, strength, joy

ASSOCIATED PHYSIOLOGY:
Metabolism & digestion

BALANCED:
Happy, powerful, confident and organised.
Strong willpower, sense of self and ambition
(a real fire in your belly!), the confidence to
trust your gut instinct.

UNBALANCED:
Insecure and/or lack self-esteem.
Overly critical, stubborn or controlling,
lack a sense of purpose. Too controlling
and dominating. Anxiety, stomach pain,
intestinal contraction, abdominal pain,
IBS and digestive issues.

HOW TO ALIGN
Spend time in the sun and whisper positive
affirmations to yourself. Try heat-building
yoga poses that engage your abs, weight
training and boxing or martial arts to
improve your sense of inner power.

HEART
Anahata

Twelve Petal Lotus

LOCATION
Centre of the chest

ELEMENT
Air

CRYSTALS
Chrysoprase, jade, rose quartz, rhodochrosite, bloodstone, malachite, ruby fuchsite

KEY WORDS
Love, compassion, emotional balance, calmness, serenity

ASSOCIATED PHYSIOLOGY:
Immune system, heart & blood

BALANCED:
Loved and loving

UNBALANCED:
Colds, flu, heart and lung issues, high/low blood pressure, poor circulation, asthma, breathing difficulties. Codependent, needy, distant, jealous, self-critical. Shy, lonely, anxious or depressed. Lack of forgiveness and empathy.

HOW TO ALIGN
Try performing a 'loving-kindness' meditation. Increase your intake of green vegetables and take lots of walks in nature. Generate a love for the environment and seek out sustainable lifestyle choices. Hug more. Be kind to yourself. Take time to practise self-care.

THROAT
Vishuddha

Sixteen Petal Lotus

LOCATION
Above the collarbone

ELEMENT
Ether

CRYSTALS
Sodalite, turquoise, aquamarine, kyanite, amazonite, larimar, blue apatite, blue lace agate

KEY WORDS
Communication, expression, guidance, inner truth

ASSOCIATED PHYSIOLOGY:
Express yourself freely and easily

BALANCED:
Express yourself freely and easily

UNBALANCED:
Sore throat, mouth ulcers, gum disease, tonsillitis and thyroid issues. Argumentative, too loud or too quiet, ignorant, offensive, unassertive and dishonest. Hesitation in expressing emotions or voicing opinions, overly opinionated, lacking vocabulary, often being misunderstood.

HOW TO ALIGN
Wear blue crystal pendants and necklaces. Try some neck stretches and yogic breathing exercises (Lion's Breath is a particularly good one). Get in the habit of expressing yourself more through personal style or actions. Give journalling a go and sing your heart out.

THIRD EYE
Ajna

Two Petal Lotus

LOCATION
Between the eyes/brow

ELEMENT
Light

CRYSTALS
Amethyst, sugilite, blue sapphire, labradorite, Iolite, lapis lazuli, fluorite

KEY WORDS
Spiritual awareness, intuition, psychic power, focus, mental clarity

ASSOCIATED PHYSIOLOGY:
Hormones, pituitary & pineal glands, brain & eyes

BALANCED:
Calm, meaningful dreams, intuitive, plans ahead, perceptive.

UNBALANCED:
Eye problems, headaches, migraines, insomnia, brain disorders. Overwhelming emotions, disassociation or hallucinations. Impatience or negative thoughts. Lack of imagination, poor vision and memory, obsessions, unable to visualise, fixed mindset.

HOW TO ALIGN
Meditate while holding a crystal to your brow. Try some inverted yoga poses, such as Plough Pose. Enhance your diet by eating purple foods, such as grapes and blackberries. Tap into your intuition and give it a workout with some visualisation and manifestation exercises.

CROWN
Sahasrara

Thousand Petal Lotus

LOCATION
Top of the head and several inches above

ELEMENT
Spirit

CRYSTALS
Amethyst, lepidolite, clear quartz, diamond, rainbow moonstone

KEY WORDS
Consciousness, enlightenment, unity, peace, transcendence

ASSOCIATED PHYSIOLOGY:
Biological cycles

BALANCED:
Spiritually content, feels at one with the universe. Forgives, shows compassion and empathy and is altruistic.

UNBALANCED:
Poor coordination, chronic headaches, exhaustion. Cynicism or apathy, addicted to spirituality, self-destructive tendencies, megalomania and hubris. Lack of direction and goals, desire to oversleep.

HOW TO ALIGN
Use associated crystals to help unlock this gateway to the soul. Try meditation and energy-shaking exercises such as cardio and yoga. Cut down on your intake of sugars and processed foods. Focus on rest and achieving a good amount of sleep – set up a healthy sleep routine. Avoid toxic relationships.

How to heal
WITH CRYSTALS

Now that you are acquainted with crystals
and their healing powers, it's time to put their
therapeutic energies into practice

The easiest way to harness the healing power of crystals is to incorporate them into your life and keep them in close contact with you. There are simple ways to do this, such as wearing them on your clothes close to specific chakras or as jewellery (see page 44) and positioning them around your home to enhance your aura (see page 64) and the flow of energy in your living space. You may also want to create a healing grid to amplify their energy.

You can incorporate crystals into your beauty routines too, and bring wellness to your everyday life. Make your own beauty water, oil mist or an elixir (see page 94), take a relaxing crystal bath (see page 91) or give yourself a crystal face massage (see page 92).

For more specific issues, learning some simple techniques, such as Reiki, can help you to engage with your crystals and really feel the impact they can have on your wellbeing. This ancient Japanese stress-reduction meditation technique involves a practitioner placing their hands on certain areas of the body, then manipulating the flow of energy within a person's body. Healing crystals can become part of the process, as their vibrational energies can help assist the flow of universal energy with which Reiki is concerned. Acupuncture techniques are another useful technique and incorporate crystals – they can even be performed on yourself. Read on and you'll be armed and equipped with all the skills you need to stay healthy with crystals!

Healing crystals can
play a number of roles
in your day-to-day life

"Learning simple techniques,
such as Reiki, can help you
to engage with your crystals"

Balance your chakras

1 Find your energy blockages

Match your symptoms to your relevant chakra. Depending on which one is blocked, you will be feeling a certain way. Once you've determined which chakras are out of balance or blocked, you can work towards healing them.

2 Pick your crystals

Locate relevant crystals. The easiest way to do this is to find a crystal in each chakra colour. For the areas you feel are out of whack, put more thought into which crystals to pick. If your stomach is feeling out of sorts and blocked up, go for a highly-energising crystal in as bright an orange as possible – such as orange calcite. If you are struggling with an overactive bowel, perhaps go for something more grounding, such as a tiger's eye.

3 Prepare

Cleanse and activate your crystals. Make sure you adhere to the needs of each crystal, whether that is cleansing with smoke or water or otherwise. For sacral chakra, you might want to charge the crystal by moonlight, while solar plexus crystals will prefer to absorb solar energy.

4 Lie down

Find a quiet place where you will not be disturbed, and lie down flat on your back (in Savasana, aka Corpse Pose). Either by yourself, or with the help of a friend, place the relevant crystals on the chakra area.

5 Relax

Breathe slowly, taking deep inhales and long exhales, for five minutes. While you lie there, visualise the chakra you feel needs most work healing itself.

6 Focus

After five minutes determine how you are feeling. Do you feel like anything has changed? It may be the case that you need a couple more sessions in order to feel better.

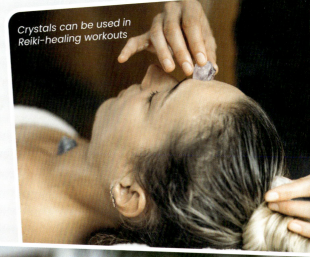

Crystals can be used in Reiki-healing workouts

Chakras can help to rebalance the body

Using a crystal wand

Crystal wands are an essential tool for anyone who is serious about healing with crystals

A crystal wand has two ends: the rounded end, which can be used for massage, and a pointed end, which is used to apply pressure to reflexology and acupuncture points in order to stimulate certain organs, help alleviate stress and offer instant pain relief. Here are a few techniques to try out yourself.

Acupuncture with a crystal wand

1 For headaches and colds

Gently rub the larger end of the crystal along the base of the back of your skull to relieve neck tension. Feel for the grooves at the top of your neck, where the skull and neck meet, and provide gentle pressure with your thumbs. Then use the narrower end of the wand to gently apply deeper pressure in these two grooves.

2 For stress, facial pain, toothaches and neck pain

Roll the side of the wand down from the side of your neck, below the ear, and along the shoulder. Press the end of the wand into the shoulder well acupressure point muscle on your shoulder, where the curve of your neck ends. Be careful not to put any pressure on the bone. Repeat on the other side.

3 For lower back pain

Place your hands on your hips and feel for the top of your buttocks with your thumbs. Perform a sacral rub with a crystal wand by pressing the larger end into the dents approximately two finger-widths from either side of your spine, to the side of your tailbone. Rub in a circular motion in the sensitive area above your buttocks, approximately in line with your hip bones. Be careful not to put any pressure on the bone. Also try using the larger side of the wand to rub your gluteus medius, beneath your hip bone. This can ease the hip flexor and aid in sciatic pain.

4 For chest congestion, coughs and breathing problems

Rub a crystal 2.5 centimetres (one inch) beneath the collarbones, in the groove beside the breastbone, before the first rib. Gently press the larger end of the wand into the groove, building up to firmer pressure. Repeat on the other side.

REIKI-INSPIRED HEALING WITH A CRYSTAL WAND

Crystal wands can also be used when it comes to Reiki-style energy work.

1. Hold the wand over the problematic area of the body, and draw a spiral in the air, moving in a counter-clockwise direction.

2. Hover the wand over the area, and visualise high-vibration healing energy coming through the crystal. By doing this, the targeted area will be recharged with positive energy.

3. Point the wand away from the body when you are done. This will have the effect of drawing energy away from the body.

Tumbled stones, pyramids and towers can also be used for this.

Crystals for YOUR HEALTH

Discover the best crystals for improving your health and wellbeing, whatever your issue may be

Crystals for men

While perhaps more associated with women's health, there are in fact a range of crystals that can help men with their fertility and general wellbeing

t's no secret that when it comes to matters of the heart (or head), men can often find it difficult to open up about their feelings, doubly so when what is troubling them relates to their fertility and potential hormone imbalances.

As with women, men can be affected by a range of physical and psychological ailments that can have a major impact on their wellbeing and mental health. Infertility can be a particularly difficult obstacle to face. Approximately one in six couples trying to conceive experience fertility issues, with male infertility accounting for 25 percent of cases.

Another common occurrence is erectile dysfunction (ED). Affecting around ten percent of men, ED can be caused by stress or depression, but it is more commonly the result of a physical problem, and it can in fact be a symptom of male hormone imbalance.

Often dismissed as ageing, hormonal imbalances in men can result in fatigue, hair and memory loss, and a low sex drive, among other symptoms. However, as with all of the issues mentioned here, there are means by which they can be alleviated, and while we are not suggesting that they are ever a substitute for seeking professional medical help, crystals can provide a variety of solutions.

PYRITE
Solar plexus chakra

BEST FOR
Increasing fertility and boosting male energy

Known as 'fool's gold', pyrite is an iron sulphide that was once used in firearms. Thankfully it also has less lethal uses, including memory stimulation, enhanced willpower and protection against pollutants and negativity.

TIPS
Put pieces by entrances to fend off bad energy and attract good fortune

CHRYSOPRASE
Heart & sacral chakras

BEST FOR
Low sperm count

Home to traces of nickel, this marvellous little gemstone encourages detoxification and helps to create hormonal balance. It's also said to be able to mend a broken heart and heal the scars of childhood by helping people to release emotions they may have buried in their youth.

TIPS
Place under your pillow to enhance your night's sleep

SMOKY QUARTZ
Root & solar plexus chakras

BEST FOR
Sexual dysfunctions

Smoky quartz is a power stone known to help with a range of problems including impotence, infection, warts, tumours and even cancer. By helping to dispel negative energy and toxins, it fosters a sense of both inner and external tranquillity.

TIPS
Allow to absorb moonlight for 8-12 hours for a powerful charge and balanced cleanse

BLUE PIETERSITE
Third eye & solar plexus chakras

BEST FOR
Impotence, blood pressure

Said to be lucky, this stone of truth can help men struggling with impotence or a hormonal imbalance. It also supports the endocrine system and magnifies your dreams and your ability to recall them.

TIPS
Combine with purpurite for mental clarity and insight

Crystals for women

Whether battling PMS or the menopause, crystals can ease a range of issues and soothe the symptoms of common ailments

Let's face it – being a woman isn't always easy. Dealing with that time of the month can be tricky enough for many, especially if they experience heavy bleeding, cramps or bouts of PMS. Period cramps are the result of uterine contraction, which is sparked by prostaglandins – substances similar to hormones that are linked to pain and inflammation, whereas PMS is the result of hormonal changes and can lead to headaches, acne, mood swings and tender breasts. The latter shares similar symptoms to hormonal imbalance, which can also manifest as weight gain (or loss), increased blood cholesterol and dry skin, to name a few side effects. However, these are far from the only challenges that Mother Nature can serve up.

Countless women struggle with fertility problems, which can have a wide variety of underlying causes. These can include biological troubles such as polycystic ovaries, fibroids and endometriosis, and drug-induced (both medicinal and recreational) difficulties. Aspirin and ibuprofen, taken in high doses or for an extended stretch of time, can reduce fertility, as can using marijuana.

A challenge that all women will eventually confront is the menopause. Usually beginning between the ages of 45 and 55, it can be brought on early by a woman's genetic makeup, as well as certain types of cancer treatment or surgery. Symptoms can last for years, ranging from anxiety and brain fog to irregular periods (that will eventually cease), hot flushes and mood swings.

As previously mentioned with regards to men's health, crystal healing is not intended as a direct replacement for medical advice from your GP, but it can certainly help to alleviate a lot of the symptoms connected to these female struggles. Let's take a look at how crystals can aid in the fight against a variety of problems.

> *"Aspirin and ibuprofen, taken in high doses or for an extended stretch of time, can reduce fertility, as can using marijuana"*

BLOODSTONE
ROOT CHAKRA

BEST FOR
Heavy menstrual bleeding

Rather appropriately, the bloodstone neutralises toxins in the bloodstream, soothes heavy menstrual bleeding and can counteract the impact of anaemia. It's also thought to help with low energy and brain fog.

TIPS
Wear against your skin to direct healing vibrations to where they are most needed

WHY NOT TRY?
When you are struggling with PMS and cramps, try wearing a moonstone or labradorite necklace to help balance your hormones. Also try a chrysocolla or malachite crystal around your neck on an extra long chain, on your belt or in your front trouser pocket so they can work their magic on cramps and discomfort within your womb and abdomen.

TANGERINE QUARTZ
Sacral chakra

BEST FOR

Sexual healing, body issues, sensuality

·

This uplifting crystal releases any past sexual shame and trauma, helps you to let go of any body issues and boosts self-confidence and libido.

·

TIPS

Place upon your sacral chakra or beneath your mattress in order to ignite your sexual passion and restore sexual confidence and self-love

CHRYSOCOLLA
Throat & heart chakras

BEST FOR

Blood pressure, period cramps

·

Derived from the Greek 'Chrysos' (gold) and 'Kola' (glue), this all-rounder can lower blood pressure. It can also remove period cramps, regulate blood sugar and digestion, clean the lungs and fight off infections and fevers.

·

TIPS

Store away from anything that could scratch it

BRONZITE
Sacral & root chakras

BEST FOR

Infections, iron absorption, natural cycles

·

Helping to ward off infection, cast nervous energy aside and boost iron assimilation, this crystal empowers decisive action and mental clarity. It also reflects negativity back at the source.

·

TIPS

Carrying a piece will empower you to stand up to others

MALACHITE
Third eye, heart & solar plexus chakras

BEST FOR
Cramps and contractions

Hailed as the 'midwife's stone', this crystal has strong ties to bold feminine energy, helping with menstrual cramps and pregnancy, especially when it comes to contractions. Another trick is its ability to amplify surrounding energy, whether it's negative or positive.

TIPS
Real malachite boasts concentric circles and is a mixture of blue and green

WHITE MOONSTONE
Crown chakra

BEST FOR
PMS, infertility, pregnancy

Representing the full moon and connected to the Goddess energy, divine femininity and cycles, moonstone can lessen the intensity of PMS symptoms, lift fertility and encourage hormonal balance. It can also ease the physical tolls of pregnancy and, when the time comes, labour.

TIPS
Position on your third eye chakra for optimum healing

KUNZITE
Crown & Heart Chakras

BEST FOR
PMS, reproductive issues, migraines

The pink hue of kunzite is connected to devotion and love, so it's fitting it helps both the heart muscles and circulation. It can also help the symptoms of PMS or reproductive difficulties. Soothing migraines and guiding the recovery from stress are additional attributes.

TIPS
Do not use salt water on rough kunzite as it will damage it

Crystals for mental and physical health

Since ancient times, crystals have been deployed in many forms to combat both psychological and physical imbalances, fend off negativity and foster an environment of love and creative energy

Historians estimate that humankind has been working with crystals for over 5,000 years, with references to their use in ancient Sumerian scriptures and Chinese medicines. To date more than 4,000 naturally occurring minerals (inorganic solids comprising a crystal structure) have been unearthed, so there are plenty to choose from. Many boast healing properties that have been utilised by an array of cultures throughout history, with quartz being considered one of the most effective.

Known as the master healer, this translucent crystal is mined across the globe and is famed for attracting positive energy, dispersing negativity and clearing the mind. It can be used during meditation, worn as a piece of jewellery, carried in a pocket or placed in a specific part of a home where it can radiate its energy.

Other crystals that are renowned for their healing abilities include amethyst, howlite, lapis lazuli and kyanite. Let's take a closer look at just how these crystals, along with some others, can help you to cope with a range of mental and physical issues. While we encourage you to embrace the use of crystals to help with healing, it is important to stress that they are an additional option alongside seeking professional medical advice and never a replacement for talking to a doctor.

GOLDEN HEALER QUARTZ
Solar plexus chakra

BEST FOR
Everything

This master healer has a universal ability to remove blockages and heal damage. Particularly good for anyone who feels sluggish, suffers with fatigue or chronic illness, it will amplify the energies of all nearby crystals, attracting a golden ray of healing light to everything and everyone.

TIPS
Use as a grid focus stone with clear quartz, citrine and selenite for max healing energy

LEPIDOLITE
Third eye chakra

BEST FOR
Anxiety and general anxiety disorder, bipolar disorder, premenstrual syndrome, menopause, stress, anorexia

Lepidolite boosts dopamine levels, harmonises your emotions and promotes a sense of inner calm. It also aids in transformation and release from toxic behaviours and additions as well as protecting from work stresses.

TIPS
Wear lepidolite as a talisman to maintain emotional balance

HOWLITE
Crown chakra

BEST FOR
Stress, insomnia

Specifically known for removing the frustration caused by insomnia, howlite also provides numerous physical benefits. By helping to balance calcium levels, it is great for dental, skeletal and muscular health. It is known to strengthen memory, spark a longing for further knowledge and enable awareness.

TIPS
Agate, chrysocolla and lapis lazuli work well with it

KUNZITE
Crown & Heart Chakras

BEST FOR
ADHD, detoxification and willpower

This remarkable stone can calm overactive children and adults, as well as boost affection and concentration, encourage bone development, streamline the metabolic process and push us to speak our truth. It can also help make healthy choices and detoxify.

TIPS
Put under your pillow for a night full of dreams you'll recall

RUBY
Heart & root chakras

BEST FOR
Addiction

By removing self-doubt and fostering feelings of confidence and passion for life, ruby helps focus the mind on productive tasks. A former addict imbued with energy and a new belief in their ability to avoid temptation is someone with the very best chance of ending their addiction. Improved circulation and eyesight won't hurt either.

TIPS
Wear a ruby necklace to keep the crystal close to your heart

FUCHSITE
Heart chakra

BEST FOR
Holistic health

Associated with the natural world, it can increase your green thumb, encourage you to "get back to nature" and research herbal remedies. Fuchsite inspires a sense of peace, helps you to bounce back after trauma, balances the blood, aids with carpal tunnel syndrome, spinal alignment and muscle flexibility.

TIPS
Keep it near other crystals to transfer their energies

PYROPE GARNET
Root & crown chakras

BEST FOR
Heart and blood flow

Derived from the Greek for 'fire' and 'eye', pyrope garnet stimulates blood circulation and can help treat blood disorders. A balm for heartburn, it supports the immune system, spurs sexual virility and eases the aches and pains of arthritis.

TIPS
Keep it close when meditating to reach a meditative state

LAPIS LAZULI
Throat & third eye chakras

BEST FOR
Eye health

Lapis lazuli has been prized for its appearance for thousands of years. It is good for treating a series of eye complaints, such as itching or weeping, and improves blood circulation to the eyes. Able to cool inflammation, it's also helpful for alleviating the symptoms of a migraine.

TIPS
Keep by your bed to avoid insomnia and bring dreams

SELENITE
Crown chakra

BEST FOR
Emotional healing

This crystal will soon have you standing tall, and not just because it's brilliant at dispersing negative energy and anxiety. Its key strengths lie in helping with spine alignment and strength and fixing a range of skeletal issues. It can even heal cellular damage and work to keep your skin and hair clean and healthy.

TIPS
Use a wand to cleanse your aura and remove negativity

KYANITE
Throat & third eye chakras

BEST FOR
High blood pressure; throat, brain and muscular systems; stress and sleep disorders

Connected to the throat, blue kyanite inspires connection and communication and supports the thyroid and parathyroid. Effective against fevers and muscular disorders, it also aids recovery from traumas and nurtures compassion and intuition.

TIPS
Wear as jewellery

WHY NOT TRY?

Lepidolite contains a high level of the metal lithium, which is a natural mood stabiliser, often used in treatment for bipolar disorder. Create a simple elixir by following the steps on page 94. Sip crystal infused water while at work or, during periods of stress and anxiety, add lavender essential oil to your elixir and spritz it around your space to promote calm .

Home

64

Displaying your crystals

·

72

Protecting your home

·

76

Crystals for family
& relationships

Displaying
YOUR CRYSTALS

Crystals not only fill your house with positive energy, but with a bit of thought they can add a unique decorative touch, too

When you make crystals a part of your routine, you'll soon find that their energy and power lends a new perspective to every aspect of your life, whether at home, at work or on your travels. One of the joys of crystals is their unique beauty and the sheer variety of so many stones. Obviously where you position them is important when it comes to harnessing their powers, but they are also a fantastic and attractive means of decorating your home. So not only do you benefit from their spiritual powers, but you can further enhance those powers at the same time as you add a touch of crystal beauty to your home.

Crystals aren't only an attractive option for decor, they're enormously powerful too

Displaying Inspiration

When it comes to displaying your crystals, you can make the most of their aesthetic qualities while enhancing their beneficial powers

JEWELLERY

Carry your crystals with you and show them off as a beautiful piece of jewellery. That way, you'll benefit from their power all day long.

STATEMENT PIECES

If money is no object, you can splash the cash on a dramatic statement piece and magnify the energy of your chosen crystal. These large crystals make a massive impression and a wonderful talking point to let the world know all about your passion.

CRYSTAL GARDEN

Create your very own crystal garden, either by positioning your existing crystals or by growing your own. This is a great family activity, as educational as it is exciting!

COMMAND CENTRE

A crystal command centre creates an attractive focus point for your collection. Place it in a window to keep the crystals charged and to fill your space with powerful energies.

MEDITATION SPACE

In our busy lives, we all need to take a moment to recoup our energy now and then. You can use your favourite crystals and incense, as well as other personal talismans to create a meditation space in any room of your home.

PYRAMID

Unite the energy of your crystals with the power of the pyramid by positioning your crystals within one. Whether you choose a pyramid-shaped shelf, a pyramid container or even a crystal in this unique shape, it's an attractive choice for any space.

AROMATHERAPY MEETS CRYSTAL ENERGY

Working with crystals and essential oils derived from the plant kingdom, crystal aromatherapists unite mineral and plant energies to amplify their healing aspects in every conceivable combination, bringing serenity to your home. Here are just a few options...

• Bathe with rose quartz, patchouli, rose geranium and ylang ylang to heal a broken heart.

• Spritz citrine with a combination of lemon, tangerine and yuzu to awaken creativity.

• Meditate with selenite and burn lavender, chamomile and jasmine to cultivate tranquillity.

• Really let yourself go and burn ylang ylang, cedar wood and black spruce as you dance with a piece of lapis lazuli!

Crystal aromatherapy combines powerful energies to enhance your wellbeing

An Introduction to Feng Shui

Feng shui is all about enhancing your life by placing objects in your home in a way that encourages positive energy flow, which can become even more beneficial when teamed with crystals

If you're arranging your home in line with the principles of feng shui, by putting certain crystals in the right place, you can really supercharge your feng shui experience. As the energy flows around the house and rooms, each point of the compass represents a different area of life; you can strengthen these by placing specific crystals at each compass point to add energy and focus.

Alternatively, you can take it room by room to keep things simple and use crystals alongside feng shui to bring harmony to your life.

Entrance

This is "the mouth of qi", and the place where energy enters your home. Keep it clear, clean and brightly lit and add a piece of citrine in the entrance to welcome positivity in, while popping black tourmaline near the threshold to keep unwanted energies out.

Kitchen

Make this nourishing space a welcoming one. Keep it clean, fresh and bright and treat your stove with respect, since it's symbolic of prosperity and fortune. If the kitchen is the heart of your house, selenite will make it a welcoming space that will draw visitors in.

Living room

We all love a cosy living room, but make sure that your guests can connect by placing sofas and chairs towards one another. Add clear quartz to the space to keep the energy positive and clean and all your guests and family in harmony.

Bathroom

Don't let your luck drain down the plughole by fixing leaky taps straight away. Place a piece of smoky quartz in the smallest room to balance the sometimes chaotic water energy and stabilise the atmosphere.

Bedroom

Keep your bedroom free of clutter and make sure electronics are stored elsewhere. It's all about relaxing energy here and amethyst will keep things calm. If you'd like a little romantic fizz, a piece of rose quartz on the bedside table will help things along.

By uniting crystals with the principles of feng shui, you'll be creating your very own sanctuary, surrounded by crystal energy. Refer to the compass illustration to discover what crystals can be used to enhance specific areas of your life, and where they should be placed in your home.

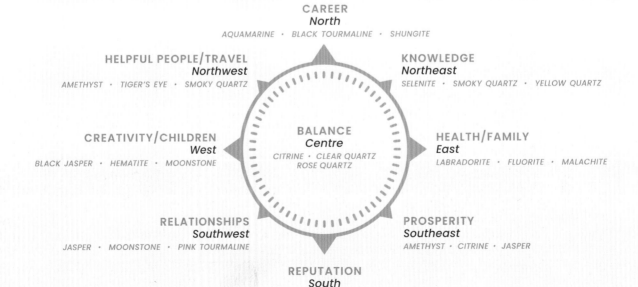

CAREER
North
AQUAMARINE · BLACK TOURMALINE · SHUNGITE

HELPFUL PEOPLE/TRAVEL
Northwest
AMETHYST · TIGER'S EYE · SMOKY QUARTZ

KNOWLEDGE
Northeast
SELENITE · SMOKY QUARTZ · YELLOW QUARTZ

CREATIVITY/CHILDREN
West
BLACK JASPER · HEMATITE · MOONSTONE

BALANCE
Centre
CITRINE · CLEAR QUARTZ
ROSE QUARTZ

HEALTH/FAMILY
East
LABRADORITE · FLUORITE · MALACHITE

RELATIONSHIPS
Southwest
JASPER · MOONSTONE · PINK TOURMALINE

PROSPERITY
Southeast
AMETHYST · CITRINE · JASPER

REPUTATION
South
CARNELIAN · FIRE AGATE · GARNET

THE BAGUA WHEEL

In feng shui, every room in the home is divided into different energy centres according to the bagua wheel, the energy map used by feng shui practitioners. Meaning "eight symbols" in Chinese, the bagua is represented by eight symbols around a centre, each of which is connected to a different part of life. You can lay the bagua map over your floor plan to identify which aspect of existence each part of your house represents and to ensure that you're making the most of the energy there.

NORTH

NORTHWEST

NORTHEAST

CAREER/LIFE PATH

HELPFUL PEOPLE & TRAVEL

KNOWLEDGE

WEST

EAST

CREATIVITY & CHILDREN

LOVE

LOVE

PROSPERITY

SOUTHWEST

SOUTHEAST

FAME

SOUTH

The bagua wheel is the energy map that governs feng shui

However you choose to display them, your crystals will work with the feng shui energy to propel it through your home

A Crystal for Every Room

Crystals are as beautiful as they are powerful, but choosing specific pieces for certain rooms can really make the best of your home

BEDROOM

Whether you're relaxing with a good book, catching up on your sleep or even enjoying some romance, you spend a lot of time in your bedroom. In this intimate space, you'll naturally want to create a place that's calm and tranquil, where you can fall asleep feeling safe and protected and enjoy the very best dreams.

•

CRYSTALS
Amethyst
Jet
Rose quartz

•

TIPS
Spray your pillow with amethyst-infused essential oils for a great night's sleep

•

Pop a piece of rose quartz on your dressing table to promote self-love

•

Keep jet beside the bed to see off nightmares

KITCHEN

For some people, the kitchen is the heart of the home. It's where the family gather, where they chat to good friends and where they prepare meals and even entertain. It's a room devoted to nourishment in every sense of the word, and a social space that's filled with life, energy and a very special sort of spark.

•

CRYSTALS
Apatite
Carnelian
Clear quartz

•

TIPS
Keep apatite in your cupboards and fridge to inspire healthy choices and prevent boredom eating!

•

Stand your hot dishes on a rest infused with carnelian to boost your creativity

•

Clear quartz will keep the busy kitchen atmosphere feeling fresh

ENTRANCES

We all want our home to be warm and welcoming and to invite in great energy, while repelling any negativity that might try to enter. With all that coming and going of entryways and hallways, it's important to keep these areas cleansed, so visitors and those who are just passing through don't leave their energy behind.

•

CRYSTALS
Garnet
Obsidian
Selenite

•

TIPS
Pop a piece of obsidian over the front door to protect the entry to your home

•

Keep garnet in your loose change pot or by the door to attract abundance

•

If you place selenite on a windowsill, you'll attract light and positivity

STUDY

With more and more people working from home these days, creating a great workspace isn't just about making sure you've got the right tools for the job. Create an environment that encourages productivity and achievement while enhancing your creativity and knowledge with crystal energy. You can even see off workplace stress and electromagnetic fields by choosing the right stones for the space.

CRYSTALS

Rainbow fluorite
Pyrite
Shungite

TIPS

A shungite coaster isn't just practical – it will repel troublesome EMF too

Keep a small piece of pyrite with your business cards to manifest prosperity

Store your pens in a fluorite pen holder to stay focused on your work

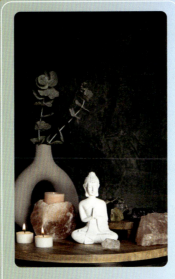

LIVING ROOM

When you have friends and visitors to your home, it's likely they'll spend a lot of time getting comfy in the living room. The key here is to create a space that's harmonious, upbeat and positive, to ward off arguments and difficult friendships. You'll also want to keep things warm and welcoming, where you can entertain with confidence.

CRYSTALS

Ametrine
Desert rose
Sodalite

TIPS

This is a great space for your crystal command centre, which is as decorative as it is powerful

Choose coasters made from slices of your favourite crystals for an attractive and practical way to encourage positive energy

A chunk of ametrine in a dark corner projects soothing light and energy while calming negative emotions

BATHROOM

Bathrooms are functional spaces as much as they are places for relaxation, so it's important that you're able to embrace both of these practical elements. With family life sometimes being chaotic, your bathroom might see a lot of foot traffic and exist in something of a whirlwind, but you can still calm that chaos and create a welcoming space to connect with yourself.

CRYSTALS

Citrine
Clear quartz
Himalayan salt rock
(keep away from water)

TIPS

Keep your toiletries in a citrine geode to wake you up every morning

A few Himalayan salt rocks in a cute basket are a nice decorative touch and you can dissolve them in a bath when you're ready to lay back and relax

Store loose bits and bobs in a rose quartz bowl to keep yourself nurtured and remind yourself to relax

Protecting
YOUR HOME

Our home is our sanctuary, and crystal energy can help create a place where we are safe, protected and relaxed

If you want to attract positivity into your home, adding crystals to your surroundings is a great way to protect yourself and create a place that's safe, nurturing and filled with the very best energies.

Which crystal should you choose?

Choosing the right crystals for each room can transform the space, whether you want to keep your bedroom tranquil or make healthy choices in the kitchen. By taking care with where you place your crystals as you set your intention, you'll not only add an attractive element to your décor, but you'll be filling your home with great energy.

Different crystals help with different aspects of life. For example, keep things relaxed and the conversation flowing with amethyst, selenite and spirit quartz. Make the best choices for your health with apatite and emerald. Stay healthy with jasper and bloodstone. Relax and unwind with moonstone or spice things up with garnet.

Keep yourself safe

Crystals aren't just for good energy, but can protect you and your home, too. Although alarms and locks provide physical security, you can add a spiritual touch by squaring off your home to guard against crime. To do this, simply place selenite in all four corners of the property while setting the intention of keeping your home and your loved ones protected, then let the crystals go to work.

Of course, negativity can come from inside the home. Whether its young children running wild, teenage attitude or just the everyday stresses of family life, you can regularly clear your living space using crystal energy. To do this, burn incense throughout the home to create a fresh atmosphere, then place crystals that promote harmony and good vibes. The Fruit of Life is a fantastic grid to create in a space used by youngsters – though make sure to place it out of the reach of young children – and choose stones tailored to the specific issue you want to deal with. It's a great activity to do with your children, so let them help to choose the crystals by listening to their own intuition.

Counteract electromagnetic fields

Electromagnetic fields (EMF) generated by modern technology are part of everyday life and some people are really sensitive to them. If that sounds like you, wearing a shielding stone such as pyrite or laying a grid placed in the room that is impacted by EMF can be a strong weapon against this exhausting energy. Simply set the grid in the corners of the room or around the specific space and let the air – and your mind – clear.

PROTECTION SYMBOLS

Using symbols such as stars and pentagrams in your home not only serves as decoration, but can provide powerful protection for your home. Whether you wear them as jewellery or lay your crystal grids in these shapes, they'll work with your intentions to keep your home and your loved ones safe.

Pentacle
This ancient symbol offers protection against evil

Five-pointed star
Repel bad energy and negativity, both from outside and within

Six-pointed star
Keeps things positive and your world in balance

Square
Harness the strength and security of this solid shape

SELENITE
Crown chakra

BEST FOR
Shielding

Selenite is an excellent energy clearer and can cleanse and charge other crystals. It is also great for creating calm. When placed around your home, it creates a protective fortress that will shield your house from negative energies and even potential break-ins!

TIPS
Place selenite on the windowsills of every room

BLACK TOURMALINE
Root chakra

BEST FOR
Absorbing negativity and EMF

Black tourmaline will absorb all negative energy around it. This means that it's excellent to have around your home to help prevent conflict and family members who often visit with criticisms!

TIPS
Keep a chunk in the most sociable areas of your home

BLACK OBSIDIAN
Root chakra

BEST FOR
Prevent psychic attacks

Just like black tourmaline, black obsidian is a negativity absorber. Favoured by Aztecs, this volcanic glass shields against bad vibes and wards off psychic and magical attacks. It also encourages truth and intuition.

TIPS
Place a piece by the door to shift any incoming negativity

A QUICK AND EASY EMF GRID

If EMFs are a problem in your home, this very quick square grid is easy to set up and can protect a space of any size. All you need are four pieces of selenite, four pieces of shungite and a flint keystone.

1. Hold each crystal in your hand and set your intention.
2. Place a piece of selenite on the inside of each corner of the grid.
3. Place a piece of shungite on the outside of each corner of the grid.
4. Place the keystone in the centre.
5. Activate your grid and let it go to work.

You can leave the grid in place for as long as it is needed, just remember to keep it charged so its powers don't wane.

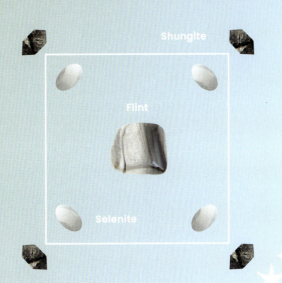

Shungite

Flint

Selenite

Crystals for
FAMILY & RELATIONSHIPS

The crystals you bring into your home will promote health, wellness and harmony for all of your loved ones.

Romantic partners

Crystals can make sure the path of true love runs smoothly... or spicily

SUNSTONE
Sacral chakra

BEST FOR
Sensuality

•

Also known as heliolite, named for the Greek solar god, sunstone embodies the sun itself – and the sun's energy is a great choice to open yourself up to new experiences and add some spice to the bedroom.

•

TIPS
Keep it on the bedside table

RED JASPER
Root chakra

BEST FOR
Reigniting the spark

•

If the spark has gone out of your relationship, red jasper re-energizes sexual organs and increases emotional stamina in a relationship, helping to improve passion and erotic desire as well as promoting longevity and stability.

•

TIPS
Wear it as jewellery

PINK OPAL
Heart chakra

BEST FOR
Honesty

•

Pink opal energy encourages us to share our true selves and make deep, romantic commitments. It can help you move forward, forgive any past mistakes and focus on hopes for the future.

•

TIPS
Display it wherever you spend quality time with your partner

EMERALD
Heart chakra

BEST FOR
Successful love

•

Emerald is associated with love and faithfulness. It is said the stone changes colour as a sign of infidelity and is used in promise rings and engagement rings. It is also a stone of protection, worn as a talisman by travellers and warriors.

•

TIPS
Wear it as jewellery, particularly as a commitment ring or lover's gift

FIRE OPAL
Sacral chakra

BEST FOR
Commitment and passion

•

All opals are long associated with love and passion. However, the fire opal is especially potent when it comes to inspiring enduring passion, bringing creativity into the bedroom as well as emotional stability.

•

TIPS
Wear it as jewellery, or place beside the bed. If exposed to too much water or sunlight, it may lose its lustre.

DID YOU KNOW?

Crystals have been used as a sign of love and devotion for centuries. In the West, the diamond in an engagement ring is a sign of everlasting love. In Victorian times, lovers would gift acrostic rings, where the first letter of each of the names of the stones in the setting would spell a word. "Dearest" was a popular choice, made from seven stones: diamond, emerald, amethyst, ruby, emerald, sapphire and topaz.

Babies, Children and Teens

For youngsters, everything is an exciting discovery, while teenagers face a unique set of challenges, but crystal energy can help guide them through

AMBER
Solar plexus chakra

BEST FOR
Teething trouble

•

Teething is a really trying time for even the happiest baby. When amber is worn against the skin, the baby's body heat will trigger the release of microscopic amounts of succinic acid. When this absorbs into the bloodstream, it soothes sore gums and bad tempers.

•

TIPS
Think about amber teething jewellery – but always supervise when in use

LABRADORITE
Third eye chakra

BEST FOR
Hormonal issues

•

Adolescence can be a trying time, but labradorite can help your teens through their most difficult moments. Since it's a stone linked with transformation, labradorite has naturally powerful properties that can help to calm turbulent hormones and in girls, bring relief from menstrual tension.

•

TIPS
Keep in a pocket or wear as jewellery

CHAROITE
Third eye chakra

BEST FOR
Neurodiversity

•

This stone has uniquely soothing powers that can help bring out hidden potential. Its calming energies focus the mind and ward off frustration and doubt at all ages.

•

TIPS
Keep in your child's room

SODALITE
Third eye chakra

BEST FOR
Anti-anxiety

•

Known as the stone of serenity, sodalite's calming properties soothe anxiety and panic at any age. It can help your child articulate their feelings, as it encourages self-expression and confidence.

•

TIPS
Carry in a school bag

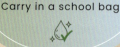

BLUE LACE AGATE
Throat chakra

BEST FOR
Creativity

This enhances focus and puts the emphasis on creativity for wellbeing. It's a serene stone, so grab a few minutes of peace while your little one creates.

TIPS
Decorate creative spaces with it

SPIRIT QUARTZ
Crown chakra

BEST FOR
Self image

A piece of spirit quartz will imbue teens with bright energies that will give their confidence a boost and banish self-doubt, building them up every single day. Its passive, positive energy.

TIPS
Keep beside your teen's mirror

RAINBOW FLUORITE
Crown chakra

BEST FOR
Exam stress and brain fog

Highly prized for its decorative qualities, rainbow fluorite will stabilise and cleanse away stress and anxiety, encouraging positivity and mental balance. It clears brain fog and reminds the teens in your life that they can transform their stress into success. At exam time, fluorite is a must.

TIPS
Carry a piece to exams and during revision

ARAGONITE
Root chakra

BEST FOR
Emotional turmoil

Aragonite is a great stabiliser, perfect for steadying teenage emotions and giving them the strength to withstand the winds of change. It helps to centre oneself, enhancing patience and accepting who you are. It also helps to temper teenage moods and remove anxiety and fear.

TIPS
Use in an elixir to aid with problematic skin and keep beside a dresser to promote self-esteem and inner peace

Loved Ones

Crystals can keep everyone feeling full of energy and vitality, ward off conflict and encourage affection, whether it's within a long-time friendship or with a difficult family member

PERIDOT
Heart chakra

BEST FOR
Repel conflict

•

Peridot resonates with healing and repels anger and envy. It transforms bad feelings into positive energy, reducing stress and making us less judgemental of ourselves too.

•

TIPS
Incorporate into jewellery

YELLOW TOPAZ
Solar plexus chakra

BEST FOR
Supportive friends

•

Yellow topaz reminds us to feel gratitude for nurturing friendships. It also acts as a beacon, bringing in kindred spirits to share the social fun.

•

TIPS
Display it in your social spaces

ANGELITE
Throat chakra

BEST FOR
Elderly relative

•

Angelite can soothe the pains and stiffness associated with bone conditions such as arthritis. It's also a good choice to help you get a great night's sleep.

•

TIPS
Wear it close to the source of discomfort

Pets

It might come as a surprise to learn that pets can feel the good vibes from crystals. Whether you want to keep them calm, make sure they're healthy and free from discomfort or just bathe them in love, there are plenty of choices, so get researching! Here's one to get started with...

MORGANITE
Heart chakra

BEST FOR
Compassion

•

This is a gentle stone that promotes love of all kinds. Helps to let go of things (and relationships) that no longer serve us, find compassion and forgiveness and guide us away from negative behaviours. It promotes joy and openness, leading to successful, authentic relationships of all kinds.

•

TIPS
Keep in your pocket

BROWN AGATE
All chakras

BEST FOR
Everything

•

Whether you're a cat or dog person, or keep rabbits, goldfish or animals of any size, brown agate is a great all-rounder. This stone enhances strong physical foundations to keep your friend powering through the day and it's got great grounding properties too, meaning your pet will always feel secure and surrounded by love.

•

TIPS
Attach it to a collar, above a cage or wherever your pet pals will feel the benefit

Lifestyle

84
Living with crystals
·
90
Crystals for self-care
·
98
Crystals for work
·
100
Travelling with crystals

Living
WITH CRYSTALS

People are often unsure as to how they might incorporate crystals into their lives, but once you start you'll wonder how you ever managed to live without them!

E instein famously stated that "everything is energy and that's all there is to it", but what happens when that energy becomes blocked or, even more worryingly, turns negative? Those who have already discovered the potency of crystals know exactly what to do and with a few handy hints, you too can harness the awesome power of crystals. It's hard to imagine how a geometrically regular formed lump of homogeneous solid substance could change a life for the better but millions of people the world over have found that they do, simply by allowing them to assist in their flow of energy.

So, how do you bring crystals into your life?

The answer is 'through daily rituals' and the good news is that it's incredibly easy to do. We all carry out little rituals day in day out, whether consciously or unconsciously, but these repeating behavioural patterns can easily take on magical significance if they are completed with crystals.

"With a few handy hints, you too can harness the awesome power of crystals"

Burn sage to purify the air around your crystals to remove the imbalances they pick up from the environment

Find yourself flustered at work or easily distracted by the noisy telephone conversations on the neighbouring work station? By decluttering your desk and adding a piece of fluorite you can promote clarity and enhance your productivity. If you need a little pick-me-up, place some citrine by the front door and every time you leave the house, make sure you pop that joyous yellow crystal in your pocket for a happy and fun-filled day.

Crystals everywhere!

Every aspect of your life can be improved by turning your daily activities into beautiful miniature crystal-infused ceremonies.

TIME TO GROUND

Before you begin your daily crystal rituals, it's important that you take the time to ground yourself. Ideally you want to let your head float in the clouds while keeping your feet firmly planted on planet Earth! By grounding yourself you will be more focused, centred, and present in the here and now. When searching for an appropriate grounding crystal it's always best to look at those of a red, black or brown hue. Once you have chosen the perfect crystal, clasp it in your left hand and concentrate on the feel of it against your palm. As you breathe deeply, repeat the affirmation 'I am here, I am rooted and connected to the Earth, I am grounded'. Wear a smoky quartz against your skin to remain grounded all day long.

Also known as schorl, black tourmaline is the perfect crystal to ground yourself with – its strong energy can easily dispel negative vibrations.

Meditating with Crystals

Whether you are seeking spiritual enlightenment, wishing to harness Earth's natural powers or simply looking for some peace and tranquillity, meditation can help you achieve your goals. It could be argued that all you need to reach the threshold of inner peace is you and your ability to calm those ever-intrusive thoughts, but many people have discovered a way to enhance their meditation experience by incorporating crystals into their ritual. It is particularly useful for those who have never meditated before and need that extra boost to help them concentrate, not to mention the fact that everything is more beautiful and magical when crystals are involved!

While in a relaxed state, most people find that they are far more open to the world around them. The universe is a web of pulsing energy and as you drift into a meditative state you will become aware of this connectedness. Crystals act as a focal point, enabling you to pierce through the noise of everyday life. The right crystal can support your desires and help you to hear your inner voice. The power of the Earth will be amplified and, when you become more adept at quietening your thoughts, you may be fortunate enough to hear the 'voice' of your crystal. In this way you can let go of the unnecessary hubbub inside your brain and focus on what is truly important.

EVERYDAY RITUALS

How to invite the power of crystals into your everyday routines

- If you already do yoga then you know the calming benefits, but why not enhance the experience by incorporating crystals into your exercise regime? Place a beautiful amethyst on your yoga mat as you perform your relaxing movements. By adding crystals into your yoga ritual you will find that it amplifies the soothing aura.

- Everybody knows the importance of drinking enough water but by creating gem water you can turn a bland drink into an effortless crystal ritual. Simply pop some black tourmaline into a pitcher of fresh spring water and leave it in the fridge overnight. In the morning, take out the crystal and sip your elixir all day long to keep those negative energies at bay.

- Sometimes we need a confidence boost to get us ready to face the day. By warming an aragonite star cluster in your hand as you choose what you want to wear, the positive energy will infuse throughout your body and make it feel fabulous.

Crystals come in a myriad of breathtaking colours and shapes, each one a gift from Mother Nature

Try this simple exercise to meditate with crystals:

1 Choose an appropriate crystal. This will depend on your reasons for meditating. You should always ask your crystal for permission to work with it. You may initially feel self-conscious about this step but when you start connecting with your crystal, you will soon realise that it has a life of its own.

2 Cleanse your crystal, making sure that any residual energy from previous usage has been removed.

3 Find a quiet location where you can sit upon the ground and connect with the Earth.

4 Turn off your phone and make sure that no one will disturb you. This is YOUR time.

5 Allow your eyes to drift shut.

6 Think about your breathing and monitor it as you breathe in and out, in and out…

7 Clasp your crystal in your hand and gaze into its soul with your mind. Imagine you are looking into its very core, even though your eyes are shut.

8 Focus on your intentions but be receptive to the messages emanating from your crystal too.

9 When you are ready, reconnect with your breathing and gently open your eyes.

10 Don't forget to thank your crystal for sharing its energy with you.

Crystal spirits

Once you have become adept at meditating with crystals you may be able to connect with the spirit that lies within its heart. Each crystal has a personality and, with practice and perseverance, you can learn to hear the messages locked inside. Here is the best way to bond with your crystal spirit:

"The right crystal can support your desires and help you to hear your inner voice"

CHOOSING THE RIGHT CRYSTAL

Take time to pick the perfect crystal for your meditative needs since every crystal packs a different punch. Aventurine and smoky quartz will promote a sense of peace while also decreasing stress. Amethyst will heighten your intuition. Need pepping up? Focus on some selenite or citrine. If you're suffering from a broken heart or on the lookout for a new love then incorporate rose quartz into your meditation session. Make sure that you have chosen the crystal that aligns with your needs. If you are unsure, hover your hand over your collection and let the crystal choose you.

The delicate mint green aventurine will bring you inner peace

- Follow the basic steps to calm your inner voices.
- Now imagine that you are staring into the crystal.
- Push your way through the surface and start walking towards its centre.
- Imagine a door right at the heart.
- Focus until the door begins to open.
- Whoever steps through the door will be the crystal spirit.
- Make its acquaintance and know your crystal's true nature.

Crystals for SELF-CARE

Can crystals jumpstart your sex life, give you great skin and make you feel a million dollars? The following practices, often rooted in increasing self-worth, may set you on the right track...

Crystal usage has always gone hand in hand with the domains of beauty, romance and even sex. After all, no matter how you live your life, your outward and self-image, and the way you relate to others, is always a worthy place to focus the healing energies and sense of balance that crystal practices can help flourish.

Beauty and trends

While the use of crystals in beauty products stretches back thousands of years, in recent years, the market has seen a real boom. Items like gua sha rollers are seen frequently on videos by beauty influencers, but walk around your pharmacist and you'll equally see crystals featuring on the ingredients lists of everything

SELF-CARE CRYSTALS

Sugilite
A purifying stone of love, sugilite promotes self-awareness and spiritual transformation by awakening the third eye and crown chakras. It attracts positivity and brings a sense of comfort and stability.

Jade
This calming stone is associated with the heart, but also the emotional intelligence of ageing. It's thought to have anti-inflammatory properties for skin and hormonal glands, to smooth facial tensions.

Rhodochrosite
Essential for emotional healing, oozing nurturing love, self-love and compassion, it provides balance and a connection to Mother Earth and universal love as well as having a detoxing effect on the physical body.

Opal
The shimmering colours of this stone are associated with passion, youthful liveliness and flirtation. It's thought to also be stimulating for skin, nail growth and general strengthening of the body and spirit.

Rutilated quartz
Thought to work well with water due to its vibrational conductivity, rutilated quartz is great for bathtime relaxation sessions. The rutile inclusions promote positivity and regenerate damaged cells.

from exfoliators, hair and face masks to perfumes and foundations or blushers. As ever, if you're invested in the metaphysical aspect of the crystal practice, be wary of cheaply produced imitations (eg coloured glass) or, on the flipside, products that seem to make grand claims for a high price and little return. These may not necessarily be unsafe to use, but good quality/value is never a bad thing in something you may use daily in close contact with your face and body!

Using elixirs

There is a lot to be said for taking the DIY route when it comes to self-care treatments in the crystal realm: not only do you then get the benefits of the treatment itself, but it can also bring a strong sense of mindfulness in these occasionally soulless everyday tasks. In that spirit, the production of elixirs (as explored overleaf) is a great method to incorporate your newfound crystal knowledge.

Sex, relationships and fertility

Another huge topic, but another area where small rituals can go a long way. Here we'll explore some of the crystals that are most commonly associated with how we think about our sex lives in all of its many colours and take a look at some of the latest shopping and online trends in this domain – from the mindful, to the hands-on and some aspects to be weary of.

Crystal Bathing

The thought process behind incorporating crystals into your bath-time routine is not just about relaxation (although it's part of it!). Water's conductive nature is also thought to help amplify the subtle processes at the core of healing crystal exercises. Bathtime is also, obviously, a great moment to immerse yourself in these techniques because a) you're at your most relaxed and open and b) whatever you're feeling gets amplified – both metaphorically and, some say, metaphysically.

1 Choose your crystal

Crystals from the quartz family are highly rated for water activities due to their conductivity and they're less likely than others to splinter (although some compounds might). The usual warnings about checking for supplier safety assurances apply if you're planning to submerge the crystal.

2 Rinse your crystals

Ideally you will have charged the crystal, using methods outlined elsewhere, but it's also good to give them a

quick wipe down of any dust or other debris that might have settled on them.

3 Run your bath

Get the water to a temperature that you're comfortable in, add essential oils, light a candle as desired. Playing crystal bowl music on a (splashproof) sound device can help heighten the crystal's frequencies and general atmosphere – you can find compilations on YouTube, SoundCloud or other streaming services.

4 Arrange your crystals

If you've got a selection of different coloured stones and a clear bath ledge (many of us accumulate tubs and tubes here, but a good cleanout can help mindfulness), placing these around the body in a way that corresponds to your chakras can be a nice touch.

5 Crystals in the water

If you've just got a small handful of non-toxic tumblestones (or just one special one), you can either place these at the bottom of the bath (loose or in a little bag if you're worried they'll slip down the drain) or hold them in your hands or place on your body in a strategic place.

6 Visualisation and breathing

You may not want – or be able – to sustain a full 20 minutes or half hour of serious focus while enjoying a well-earned bath, but taking some moments to concentrate on breath, do a body tension check-in and saying aloud your hopes and wishes for the ritual can, some believe, help the crystals transmit and retain positive vibrations and energies.

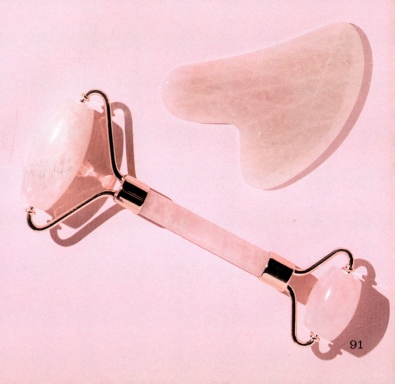

Massage for Lymphatic Drainage

ua sha is an ancient Chinese massage technique. Traditionally this could be quite a brutal practice, but luckily, for today's purposes, it usually refers to something much more gentle, involving the firm but relaxing application of a specially selected tool to the face and neck in key areas to encourage release of tension and stimulation of blood flow along the lines of your lymphatic drainage system. The process can be used casually for a quick boost, or as part of a longer relaxation session. And the tools involved can vary from the purpose-made (eg a shaped disc or roller) to the ad hoc (such as spoons or clean coins) but here we'll focus on those made from crystals which, as we've seen, can add an extra dimension of healing to the act.

You'll need
• **Moisturiser or facial oil**
Shop bought or create your own elixir-based one.

• **A gua sha facial tool**
Often jade, rose quartz or amethyst.

1 Prepare skin and tool
Your face and neck should ideally be squeaky clean, so give them a quick wash and ideally remove jewellery too. Disinfect your chosen tool with soap and water, and if it's a crystal-based product, charge it using the sunlight/moonlight techniques discussed elsewhere.

2 Apply oil or moisturiser
Use a product that agrees with your skin to act as a smooth base for the massage. The biggest stipulation is to allow movement of the tool.

3 Set an intention
If applying this technique becomes a habit, you may forget this step, but making an effort to say aloud, or to yourself, a quick summary of your aims in using the crystal – or even a quick word of self-love – can help you get a lot more out of the massage and healing crystal experience.

4 Upper face and eyes
Apply your tool in a sweeping movement from the centre of your face to your ears, lifting the skin, doing the left side of your face first, and then right. If you're using a flat object, use a forgiving angle rather than digging in, especially if you have problem skin.

5 Eyes, brows and nasal bridge
Sweep gently over the eye sockets, T-zone (where some say your third eye lives!) and brows with the larger end of the rolling tool if using one, and use the smaller end carefully to massage below the eye. Try not to nudge contact lenses out of place if you are wearing them!

6 Lower face and neck
For your chin, lips and jawline, take the same approach of moving from the centre up to your ears and temples. For the neck, you can start from the jawline and work down to the clavicle, but again, work in lines from the centre to the right and the reverse for the left to keep a nice flow going.

Using crystals in your bath-time and beauty routine can charge the atmosphere with positivity

DIY crystal-infused elixir

Learning to make crystal essences – also known as elixirs – unlocks a whole range of activities using healing crystals, from bathing to skincare spritzes or balms and even consumable tonics. Each crystal, as we know, brings its own healing properties and vibrations, but the core process is simple, and allows for customisation to your own needs. We're looking at two methods here – indirect and direct preparation of crystal-infused water or liquid. Specific healing qualities are just one element of your selection process. You are also strongly advised to research potential toxicity of the stones you have selected, and if in any doubt, use the indirect method to avoid potential contamination. .

You'll need
- **Your chosen tumble stone (from a reputable seller)**
- **1/4 cup of distilled or bottled water**
- **1/4 cup of vodka (or unflavoured spirit)**
- **A large jar (or other clean sealable container)**
- **A smaller, clear sealable container (eg a jar) for indirect method**
- **(Optional) Essential oil for fragrance**

1 Select your ingredients
When picking your crystal, consider the healing qualities of the stone, whether the crystal can crumble in water, and if it has come from a reliable maker.

2 Cleansing the crystal
You can use a sage smudging tool or other method to cleanse the crystals (see page 20). Charging of the crystals is part of the process.

3 Set an intention
In line with the purpose of the stone, make a point of saying to yourself, or out loud, what you hope to achieve from using the elixir. For example, for a bathing ritual: "I hope to soothe my skin after a hard week and relieve tension". The purpose of this is to focus your mind on the task as well as manifest the action on a spiritual level.

4 Infusing your gems
For non-toxic crystals, you may now undertake the 'direct' method of infusing the water. Add the stones to the container of water and put it in a place that catches sun or moonlight. One hour will do but overnight is also fine. For crystals of unconfirmed origin or toxicity, use the indirect method. Take a small, clear, sealable container and add your crystals. Seal it and place it within a larger container of water. Leave this to absorb sunlight or moonlight.

5 Transfer the liquid
When the charging period is over, take the stones and put them aside for recharging and reuse, and transfer the liquid to a jar. Add the vodka or spirit.

6 Prep the dropper/spray bottle
Prepare a solution of three parts water to one part of the newly created 'essence' and enjoy. You can either add a number of drops (be cautious of amount and safety) to an edible liquid or foodstuff to consume, or add it to balms, sprays or oils.

Once you know how to create a crystal elixir, you can apply it in many different ways

Crystals and Sexual WellBeing

The use of crystals in the realm of sex is all about slowing things down, getting to know yourself and feeling good vibrations from head to toe

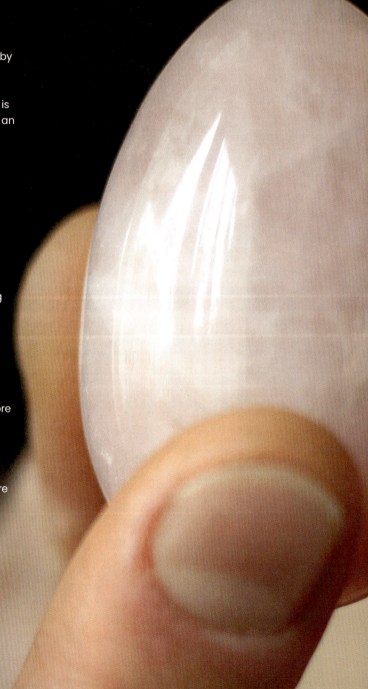

The use of crystals in sex toys has a reputedly ancient history, with claims that the practice goes back to settings such as ancient China, where jade 'yoni' (aka vaginal) eggs were thought to have been employed in such lofty domains as the Royal Palace by empresses and concubines. Whether such tales are myths spun to tantalise, or are actually the sacred, time-honoured rituals some claim, what we do know is that crystal-based love potions and tricks come with an ethos of heightened aesthetics and multi-sensory, 'slowed down sensuality'.

One thing's for sure: from luxurious obsidian wands and butt plugs that could double as high-end bookends, to elixirs that purport to enhance your prowess, these are products that take sex and body mindfulness seriously; and that's something, some argue, that's never a bad thing.

Safety is sexy

While crystal-based self-love can be game-changing for some, here are some pointers for doing it in an informed way:

- **Seek outside advice** If you're pregnant, have been fitted with an IUD or have health conditions like recurrent UTIs or low immunity, it's important to discuss your plans with a medical professional before making purchases.

- **Certified for love** Some substances are porous, potentially toxic and prone to harbouring bacteria. Many sellers offer assurances that 'virgin' crystals are employed in production. But if in doubt, adding a condom is a good option for avoiding nasty side effects down the line.

There are many enthusiasts of yoni eggs, but you should carry out some research before using to make sure they are the best option for you

- **Mother Earth** To truly connect with the Earth, as healing rituals seek to do, we have to shop mindfully. Sadly, as with all products involving mineral resource extraction, labour exploitation has been in the news. However, sellers such as Chakrubs and Yoni Pleasure Palace have gone on record to say that they use ethical practices in production.

- **Listen to your instincts** Some sexual issues cannot be resolved with the techniques listed here. If you feel pressured to engage in sexual activities that aren't working for you, these methods are no replacement for medical advice, prescribed medicines or a trip to a licensed therapist.

"Crystal-based love potions and tricks come with an ethos of heightened aesthetics and multi-sensory, 'slowed down sensuality'"

CRYSTALS FOR SEX

When it comes to the sexual regions (and higher up on your heart chakras), rubies and reds are very much the go-to hues, but it's not all focused on the lower domain...

Lack of libido

FIRE AGATE · SAPPHIRE

When sexual appetite is flagging – and we're talking about physical symptoms like dryness caused by menopause as well as depleted energy and lack of romance – fire agate and sapphire are often recommended to help get you back on track. In terms of enhanced natural lubrication, products such as yoni wands offer the silky smooth experience some find lacking in other materials. Accessories like body jewellery incorporating crystals like sapphire and agate can enhance your look and bring out all-new fun and fire in your intimate time. Going a little further into the topic, elegant – and even humorous – toys that you'd find at any sex shop can be taken down a classy, crystal-themed route.

Overcoming intimacy fears

RED CALCITE · TIGER'S EYE · AMETHYST · OBSIDIAN

Sexual wellbeing is as much about the mind as it is about the body. Many of the rituals described elsewhere in this publication offer a great stepping stone to the self-assurance, high self-worth and 'inner glow' that goes hand in hand with a thriving sex life. Crystals associated with the heart chakra such as red calcite have been described as a good place to start for boosting confidence and assertiveness in the bedroom.

Fertility and sexual health

DIOPTASE · UNAKITE · MOONSTONE · SELENITE · RUBY ZOISITE

People have turned to crystals and other holistic methods when looking to start a family since time immemorial; while precautions should be taken if you think you're pregnant, many people have found reassurance in techniques that seek to open up lower chakras associated with reproductive health. Using gems such as moonstones placed in healing patterns around your abdomen (as well as other hormonal glands) is said to unblock energy flows and, fingers crossed, allow life to flourish.

Increased flexibility and prowess

GARNET · SHIVA LINGAM QUARTZ · ROSE QUARTZ · TANGERINE QUARTZ · SMOKY QUARTZ · PYRITE · RED JASPER

There are two ways of approaching this topic: the first, which we've covered, is to employ the above crystals externally in healing meditations and rituals, like bathing. More controversially in recent years, is the use of 'yoni eggs', often inserted into the vagina to bring those crystals' 'powers' to the region, helping to exercise muscles and, some say, boost orgasms. However, there have been significant hygiene and medical warnings made on this subject (many believe the muscular benefits can be achieved by 'Kegel' exercises alone). So before you go down the yoni route, make sure you research thoroughly.

Crystals
FOR WORK

Whether you need focus, good vibes or just to relieve workplace stress, the right crystals can ensure a happy day at work

BLACK TOURMALINE
Root chakra

BEST FOR
Protection, physical wellbeing, grounding, courage, positivity

•

Black tourmaline is the ultimate protection stone. This powerful crystal absorbs all the negative energy around it, from irritating colleagues to micromanaging bosses and disgruntled customers – ensuring nothing bothers you. Stress?
Go away!

•

TIPS
Don't go to work without it!

RHYOLITE
Root chakra

BEST FOR
Strength, resolutions, progress, rationality, balance

•

Rhyolite is excellent for low self-esteem. It facilitates emotional and physical rejuvenation and helps you realise your untapped potential. It will strengthen your work relationships and help you to move on from any resentments, while dealing with challenges in a calm, rational manner.

•

TIPS
Keep it on your desk to aid with work relationships and encourage success

TURQUOISE
Throat chakra

BEST FOR
Healing, communication, protection

•

Turquoise stimulates the throat chakra for peaceful and eloquent communication as well as promoting love and forgiveness. It will also aid in exhaustion, protect against conflict, silence unproductive and self-critical thoughts and promote creative inspiration.

•

TIPS
Pop in your desk or wear as a pendant for smooth communication and protection from scheming

However you earn a living, work will always bring rewards and stresses and sometimes we just can't switch off at the end of the day. Though you may not have thought about bringing crystals into your working space, doing so might just transform not only your daily nine to five, but even the rest of your career. From protecting you against difficult colleagues to increasing your productivity and sharpening your focus and drive, crystals are able to play a part at work just as they can at home. There are plenty of stones that can have a positive impact on your career, regardless of what you're looking to achieve.

DID YOU KNOW?

Black tourmaline is the ultimate all-rounder. A brilliant shield against EMF, it also inspires clear thinking, a positive mindset, altruism and creativity. A piece in your workspace will protect against EMF, if you work with anything electronic – which is most of us these days! Wear it everyday to ensure your mood doesn't get dragged down by others and don't forget to keep a chunk at home.

CITRINE
Solar plexus chakra

BEST FOR
Prosperity, invigoration, abundance

•

Known as the 'merchant's stone', as shopkeepers and traders believed it would bring abundance and prosperity. Citrine stimulates your solar plexus, inspiring strength and confidence as well as attracting optimism and manifesting success and abundance. It also offers healing from EMF damage.

•

TIPS
Keep it close to attract promotion and increase energy

GREEN AVENTURINE
Heart chakra

BEST FOR
Imagination, calmness, balance, independence, career success, perseverance

•

This green quartz has something for everyone, from dissolving negative thoughts to blocking electromagnetic pollution. It encourages perseverance, enhances creativity and helps to stabilise the mind. It promotes decisiveness, empathy and independence.

•

TIPS
Ideal for deflecting stress

CLEAR CALCITE
Crown chakra

BEST FOR
Invigoration, purification, amplification, mental clarity, energy, inspiration

•

A fantastic stone for clearing energy blocks, stagnant mindsets and negativity. It purifies and amplifies energy, invigorates the spirit and the ability to absorb information. Also attracts prosperity, facilitates action and increases motivation.

•

TIPS
When you feel stuck, place it upon your desk!

Travelling
WITH CRYSTALS

Whether you're off on a day trip or the adventure of a lifetime, taking a few stones along for the ride will ensure happy travels!

AMETRINE
Solar plexus & third eye chakras

BEST FOR
Harmony, courage, strength

Combining amethyst and citrine, ametrine brings balance and courage. Amethyst protects against accident, travel anxiety and homesickness. The 'success stone', citrine, attracts prosperity and confidence.

TIPS
Put in your car for trouble-free motoring

RAINBOW MOONSTONE
Crown chakra

BEST FOR
New beginnings, calming, purification, intuition

A stone of vision, moonstone helps you see clearly, brings balance, hope, confidence, creativity, compassion and endurance, strengthens intuition and leaves you open to possibilities.

TIPS
Take it with you on any new adventure

MOLDAVITE
Heart & crown chakras

BEST FOR
Transformation, connectivity, communication

A natural form of glass formed by a meteorite, moldavite is a powerful talisman for personal growth, spiritual awakening, protection and good fortune.

TIPS
Wear it when travelling abroad, particularly if you are on a soul searching journey!

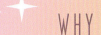

Taking a trip can sometimes be as stressful as it is rewarding, but a few crystals in your hand luggage can take care of all of that. From a hassle-free trip to calming sickness or nervousness, there are stones for even the most anxious adventurer.

By choosing the right travelling companions, you'll stay energised no matter how long you spend in the departure lounge, while even the most irate driver won't be able to dent your calm, and you'll arrive at your destination relaxed, refreshed and ready to explore: with your stones close by, even homesickness won't be a problem. Just match your intentions to your crystals, put them somewhere safe in your hand luggage and hit the road!

WHY NOT TRY?

Moldavite may help you to feel at home, but it is notoriously an intense, high vibration stone that requires some getting used to – try pairing it with one of the grounding stones (shungite or petrified wood) to balance it out if you feel a little light-headed!

"From a hassle-free trip to calming nervousness, there are stones for even the most anxious adventurer"

AQUAMARINE
Throat chakra

BEST FOR

Courage, hope, tranquility, clarity, protection

·

Aquamarine inspires a 'go with the flow' attitude and acts as a shield for your aura. Aquamarine has a deeply calming effect and helps you to take in new information by quieting the mind, clearing up confusion and inspiring wisdom and clarity.

·

TIPS

Pop it in your luggage for an ocean voyage

SHUNGITE
Root chakra

BEST FOR

Imagination, calmness, balance, independence, career success, perseverance

This mineral can only be found by Lake Onega in Russia. The high-carbon content detoxifies mind, body and spirit, while shielding you from EMF emissions (useful for travelling through airport security) and bad energies.

·

TIPS

Keep it in your hand luggage for a peaceful flight

PETRIFIED WOOD
Root chakra

BEST FOR

Invigoration, purification, amplification, mental clarity, energy, inspiration

Petrified wood is a type of fossil created by mineral preservation. Once a tree, it provides protection and a strong grounding energy. This helps you live in the moment, embrace change, face your fears and promote resilience.

·

TIPS

Keep in your pocket to control your adventure

Magic

104

The magic of crystals

·

106

Harnessing crystals to get what you want

·

114

Stars & stones

·

120

Crystal divination

The magic
OF CRYSTALS

Devotees believe all crystals have magical properties, but which are the ones that can amp up rituals and spells?

All crystals are believed to have magical properties. Practitioners of magic use what are called correspondences to find the right crystal to use in their ritual or spell. Correspondences are lists and tables that can include crystals, colours, plants, planets and much more; they're designed to help practitioners find the right tools for building a spell. They take into account an object's properties,

colour, mythological associations and more. Rose quartz, for example, with its pink colouration, gentle vibrational energy, and traditional link to Venus, is considered a perfect ingredient for romantic love spells. But for a love spell that wanted to invoke passion instead, fiery, strengthening carnelian, with its link to the sexy sacral chakra, would be a better bet.

TOP 5 CRYSTALS FOR SPELLWORK

Whether you want to dive straight into crystal magic, or you're already a magic worker who wants to introduce crystals to their practice, here are five essential stones to help with your spells.

Black Tourmaline

Black stones help to protect the spellcaster from negative energies. Try onyx or obsidian if tourmaline is out of your price range.

Moonstone

Tap into the magic of the Moon with its sacred stone. Rainbow moonstone is actually white labradorite, giving you the benefits of both stones.

Labradorite

Think of it as the equivalent of sticking an antenna on your spellcraft – mystical labradorite offers your magic a signal boost. It's beautiful, too.

Clear quartz

This do-everything stone is a great all-rounder, perfect for anyone just starting to use crystals in their spell. It's also inexpensive and easy to get hold of.

Aventurine

Green stones help nature witches attune to the power of the Earth. Jade, green onyx, malachite and chrysocolla are also good options.

While most spells and rituals that involve crystals rely on the practitioner getting the right tool for the job, there are some stones that help with magic itself, whatever its aim may be. Most spellcasters will begin their ritual by surrounding themselves with a physical and psychic circle of water, salt, and energy. Ritual magic can be a dangerous business, though; stones like onyx, obsidian and black tourmaline have powerful protective properties to help guard the would-be magician from negative energies. They could be placed at the four cardinal points of the circle or worn as a protective talisman.

Labradorite is an interesting specimen of feldspar that was first scientifically identified in Canada's Labrador region in 1770. It had long been known to the Indigenous people of the land, however. Labradorite can appear dull greeny-grey until the light hits it, when it displays its unique property of labradorescence and shimmers with an unearthly, spectral blue glow. To Labrador's Indigenous population, this was wild elemental sorcery of the Northern Lights, fallen to the cold earth and frozen into stone. Magical practitioners believe that labradorite's unique property makes it a powerful amplifier of magic, and that it can be used to enhance and boost one's own magical gifts.

Another incredibly magical stone is far more common. Clear quartz, referred to by some practitioners as the Master Healer, is also a strong amplifier. Believed to enhance creativity, wisdom and the ability to learn, as well as being associated with light and healing, it's the ideal stone for anyone wanting to get started with the magic of crystals and for anyone who feels they need a bit of a boost.

TAPPING INTO YOUR THIRD EYE

Many magical traditions have an awareness of the third eye, the intuitive sense that some believe allows us to see hidden things or scry the future. In ancient Hindu teachings, the third eye is one of seven chakras, or energy points, and the wise use of the right crystals can enhance its abilities. Try meditating with a smooth fluorite tumblestone to balance and enhance your third eye. Start by sitting and holding it, letting your physical eyes wander over and through the stone's shifting colours, and relax into contemplating them. After a couple of meditation sessions like this, try lying down with your eyes closed and placing the same stone between your brows, visualising the colour play you've previously observed in your mind and imagining your fluorite crystal as a lens that your third eye can gaze through.

Practitioners of magic believe that crystals can offer them protection, enhance their metaphysical abilities, and help them connect to the elements

"There are some stones that help with magic itself, whatever its aim may be"

Harnessing crystals to get
WHAT YOU WANT

Okay, so it's not quite that easy, but with patience and practise you too can channel crystal power to support your hopes and dreams

t seems that everybody is talking about manifesting these days but before you take your first steps along this fascinating path, you really need to take on board one vital piece of information. Manifesting is not a quick fix to solving all your problems – anyone who tells you that simply staring at a rose quartz clutched in your hand is going to bring you your very own gift-wrapped Prince Charming is either misguided or out-and-out lying. However, if you need help to plan your life goals and keep you on track, manifesting might be your answer. What's more, you don't need a pointy hat, broom or talking black cat!

Wiccans, pagans and crystal healers have long since recognised the power locked inside those beautiful rocks. Psychologists, on the other hand, have always promoted the importance of positive thinking for mental wellbeing. Put these two concepts together and you have the basics of manifesting. If you desire a financial boost you can't just wish for it and expect a winning lottery ticket to come floating down through the ceiling. Crystals are not lucky genies! However, your chances of achieving financial security increase exponentially if you create an achievable set of goals, develop a realistic game plan and, most

importantly, stay focused on those goals.

As life hurls problems at us from all directions we can be easily distracted. By manifesting our dreams on a regular basis we remain in alignment with our plans and crystals make excellent focal points.

The magic of colour
Utilising the colours of the spectrum and their corresponding intentions enable you to harness a variety of energies and invoke a magical response. The easiest way to release the desired outcome is to burn an appropriately coloured candle. You can also find the perfect coloured crystal to meditate with. The colour that catches your eye will depend upon your particular need at that time. Use the following in your own manifesting spells:

- Orange – creativity
- Red – seduction
- Yellow – abundance and joy
- Purple – intuition
- Blue – protection
- Green – renewal and earthly possessions

Your altar can be inside or out in the open – you can even share your sacred space with family and friends

Building a Crystal Altar

When manifesting, it is important that you have somewhere special to focus on your intentions. A crystal altar can be both useful and an extremely beautiful addition to your home. What's more, it's really easy and fun to create one.

You'll need

- **A table, shelf or wooden floor**
- **Two or three personal items (symbolising your intentions)**
- **Appropriate crystals**
- **Pen & paper**

1 Choosing the perfect place

It's important that you take the time to locate the right place to set up your altar. It needs to be somewhere that you won't be constantly disturbed, so not in the middle of the lounge or in a corridor! Depending on the space available, find a flat surface such as a table or floor. Ideally, this should be made of wood.

2 Picking your personal symbols

Place a few thoughtful items on your altar. These should be very personal to you and symbolic of your intentions. If, for example, you long to travel, include your old walking boots or a beautiful compass. Don't overdo it. You don't want your sacred space to become cluttered.

3 Choosing the right crystals

Now comes the fun part! There are so many beautiful crystals to pick from and it is vital that you choose a crystal that will help you to manifest your desires. Make sure that you place a large standing crystal with a pointed edge in the centre of your altar as this will bring the crystals together and amplify their vibrations. Keep pen and paper handy to write down your affirmations. Place the paper under your central crystal.

Invoke your wild side with moonstone

I f you are feeling a little hemmed in and disappointed with yourself for playing it safe, why not try this manifesting ritual to get you back in touch with your passionate, crazy alter ego? Moonstone is famously connected to the heart chakra but it can also reawaken your carefree spirit, allowing you to feel the kind of freedom you experienced as a child. Sounds exciting? Then what are you waiting for?

You'll need

- **Moonstone**
- **Smudge stick and shell**
- **Matchstick**
- **Pen & paper**
- **Soft cushion or mat**

1 Cleanse the space
Light your smudge stick. Waft the cleansing smoke around you and your moonstone until the area is devoid of negative energies. Extinguish using the shell.

2 Clarify your intentions
Think about freeing yourself of all the negative thoughts that hold you back. Now write 'No more shackles, no more doubts. I am free to be me'.

3 Time to meditate
Wrap your affirmation around the moonstone and hold tightly in your hand. Close your eyes and meditate upon your intentions. See yourself running freely.

4 Make it so
Once you have rid yourself of all doubt and are feeling energised, do one thing to take you closer to your desired outcome. Wear something daring!

Feel energised with red crystals

During the long, dark winter months it's easy to feel drained of all your energy. With no summer sun to re-energise you, why not create your own personal glowing power bank? A wishing jar filled with rich red crystals can help you to manifest the energy that you are lacking.

You'll need
- **Bell or tuning fork**
- **A clear glass jar (the bigger the better)**
- **A selection of red crystals**
- **Sunstone and clear quartz**

1 Preparing the jar and crystals
Banish any residual negative energy by ringing a bell or tuning fork close to the jar and the crystals.

2 Choosing the crystals
Many red crystals such as rubies and garnets are very expensive. Pick other red crystals such as zincite, iron quartz and jasper. Place them in the jar.

3 Amplifying the power
Add sunstone to bring warmth and clear quartz to give your jar that extra boost.

4 Wish for sunny days
Place your jar near a window where the light can shine through it. Focus on the fiery colours and imagine the warmth. Touch the crystals and allow the vibrations to energise you.

Finding Love
The Crystal Way

By focusing on a beautiful delicate pink rose quartz crystal, you can draw love into your life, whether it be self-love, romantic relationships or even mending a broken heart. It can also be used to soothe any emotional drama that is creating unwanted negative energies in your home. This negative energy can flow through the body causing a blockage in your heart chakra. This in turn creates feelings of loneliness, insecurity and a lack of compassion.

You'll need
- **Candle and match**
- **Rose quartz crystal**
- **Aventurine crystal**
- **Rhodonite crystal**
- **A clear quartz crystal**
- **A special place, preferably outdoors (beach or woodland)**

1 Finding the perfect spot
Choose a place that is sacred to you where you will not be disturbed and you can tap into the natural magic that flows freely.

2 Charge yourself with intention
Ground yourself. Breathe deeply, focusing on your intention as you chant 'I am love. I give love. I receive love'. Feel the ground beneath your feet.

3 Arrange your grid
Mindfully place the rhodonite and aventurine crystals in a circle on your chosen surface. Add the rose quartz in the centre. Now light your candle.

4 Activate the magic
Trace your clear quartz wand over the grid, drawing the magic from each crystal. Repeat the mantra 'I am love. I give love. I receive love'.

Stars
& STONES

Discover how each zodiac sign can benefit from carefully chosen crystals that mesh with their fundamental strengths and struggles, helping all of us to be our best selves

What's your sign? Whatever it is, you probably know a fair bit about it – its name and what it symbolises, its season of the year, maybe its modality – whether it's energetic cardinal, practical fixed or ever-changing mutable – and almost certainly its element, whether it's earth, air, fire or water. But did you know your star sign also has its own crystals associated with it, crystals that can help you to enhance your strengths and smooth over things that you struggle with?

When we talk about star signs we often mean our sun sign, but the signs in our horoscopes can go deeper than that. Our moon sign is the sign that the Earth's lunar companion was in when we were born, while our ascendant or rising sign is the one that was on the eastern horizon. It's easy to look these up on sites like astrology.com or cafeastrology.com; all you need is your date, time and location of birth. Moon signs tell us about our inner selves and our personal emotional lives, while rising signs tell us about the image that we project outwards to the world. To get the most from your star sign crystals, it's definitely worth finding out your moon and rising signs and looking at the crystals associated with those along with your sun sign, especially if you want a crystal to help you boost or bolster your image or imagination. You can also find out whether one sign dominates your chart (for example, if you have several planets in one sign) and look at the crystals associated with that, as your dominant sign can intersect with your sun and rising signs and influence your energy and how

you use and project it. You may find that a stone you've had an inexplicable affinity with for years is strongly related to your inner self or how you manifest your goals, or discover a new tool for helping you to achieve peace and clarity.

"Did you know your star sign has its own crystals?"

Each of the 12 signs of the zodiac can benefit from crystals associated with them or their planetary rulers, or that help those born under these signs to enhance their strengths or support things they struggle with

DISCOVER YOUR NATAL CHART

Everyone has an astrological map that is unique to when and where they were born. Once you know the date, time and location of your birth, you can figure out exactly what the stars have in store for you. There are numerous ways to find your natal chart, including online resources and books (see opposite page). Your full astrological birth chart will tell you not only your sun sign (your dominant traits) but your moon sign (your emotional personality), rising sign (social personality), and where all the planets were located when you entered this world. All these aspects can have a profound influence on who you are, who you are compatible with and what careers best suit you. If you are unsure about astrology, make sure you look up your full natal chart – you'll be amazed at the results!

· • · NATAL CHART · • · •

ARIES

SUN SIGN DATES
21 March – 19 April

·

ELEMENT
Fire

·

Aries is a cardinal sign and comes first in the zodiac, which makes the Ram a natural leader but also means they can be pushy and bossy! Frenetic and always on the go, when these high-energy individuals are in need of a little calm then amethyst is the perfect companion for some chill time. Ruled by Mars, Aries has a natural affinity with red crystals, particularly carnelian and bloodstone (heliotrope). In fact, if an individual's chart is dominated by the Ram, they can paradoxically find the normally energising carnelian soothing instead. Their traditional birthstone of bloodstone helps these high-octane folk stay grounded.

·

RECOMMENDED CRYSTALS
Carnelian · Bloodstone · Amethyst

TAURUS

SUN SIGN DATES
20 April – 20 May

·

ELEMENT
Earth

·

Solid, stubborn Taurus is a fixed earth sign and as such is primarily associated with green crystals symbolising their spring birthday, verdant gardens, fields and woods. Being lovers of luxury, Taureans are suited to their valuable traditional birthstone, emerald, but other deep green stones like malachite, green onyx and aventurine will all do in a pinch – the Bull is nothing if not practical. Ruled by Venus, they also have a strong affinity for dreamy, romantic rose quartz, which helps these sometimes inflexible individuals loosen up and embrace their sensuous side. With the Moon exalted in Taurus (it doesn't rule the sign, but it's very at home in it), moonstone offers Taureans luck and enhances their already considerable powers of attraction.

·

RECOMMENDED CRYSTALS
Emerald · Rose Quartz · Moonstone

GEMINI

SUN SIGN DATES
21 May – 20 June

·

ELEMENT
Air

·

Gemini is the mutable air sign symbolised by the Twins, and as such their minds (and mouths) move at a million miles an hour. Gemini's traditional birthstone of agate counteracts these frantic Mercury-ruled tendencies and helps Geminis to slow down and balance themselves. Agates are a type of chalcedony and come in a huge range of colours, perfect for recapturing Gemini's ever-shifting attention when they get bored – as they often do! Their zodiac neighbour Taurus's emeralds also bring them peace and equilibrium. Aquamarine, particularly if it's a cut stone so they can enjoy exploring all its facets and inner fires, helps the sometimes blunt Gemini express their thoughts to others in a kinder and gentler way.

·

RECOMMENDED CRYSTALS
Agate · Emerald · Aquamarine

CANCER

SUN SIGN DATES
21 June – 22 July

·

ELEMENT
Water

·

Cardinal Crab Cancer is the first sign of summer and the first water sign of the zodiac. Deep and defensive, Cancers sometimes show their claws, but put a moonstone into them and their tidal moods will ebb into tranquillity. Cancer is ruled by the Moon and is perhaps more in tune with its ruler than any other sign; this most lunar of crystals soothes Cancer's defensive snapping and allows them to shine their light on the world. Selenite is also associated with the Moon and its pliability is a good reminder to hard-shelled Cancer that softness is also an option. As the first of the water signs, pearls are also traditionally associated with Cancer, but care should be taken to ensure that these are sustainably sourced.

RECOMMENDED CRYSTALS
Moonstone · Selenite · Rainbow Moonstone

LEO

SUN SIGN DATES
23 July – 22 August

·

ELEMENT
Fire

·

Leo is the zodiac Lion, but it's another big cat that provides one of Leo's most beneficial crystals. Amber-gold tiger's eye is Leo's traditional stone and offers clear-sightedness, insight and protection. The king of the jungle is a fixed fire sign, which means that although they have the fiery energy of ambition and leadership, this is modulated by their fixed qualities into what can become inflexibility and autocracy. Black onyx is helpful here; its grounding qualities offer stability and help to calm the temper Leo can exhibit when it doesn't get its own way. At their best though, regal Leos are vital and joyful, and sunstone, the crystal of their ruler the Sun, helps them bestow their vibrant golden glow on the world around them.

RECOMMENDED CRYSTALS
Tiger's Eye · Black Onyx · Sunstone

VIRGO

SUN SIGN DATES
23 August – 22 September

·

ELEMENT
Earth

·

Virgo, the Maiden of the zodiac, may be an earth sign, but her mutable modality and planetary ruler Mercury makes her the most changeable of the three. Like Taurus and Capricorn, she can be solid and inflexible, but Virgo's ability to change her mind can combine with that to make her exacting and hard to please. Sapphire, the colour of the September sky, helps Virgos see the bigger picture and to let go of that unnecessary rigour. One of the reasons Virgos worry is that their deeply caring nature makes them prone to catastrophising. Their traditional stone carnelian can be a strengthening influence to keep worries at bay, while confident, courageous garnet helps alchemise their over-cautious tendencies into capable, committed energies.

RECOMMENDED CRYSTALS
Sapphire · Carnelian · Garnet

LIBRA

SUN SIGN DATES
23 September – 22 October

·

ELEMENT
Air

·

There's a superstition that only Libra, the cardinal air sign, can wear opals. For the clever, serene Scales these fiery, changeable stones, sacred to Libra's ruling planet Venus, symbolise the constant fluctuation required to maintain balance and equilibrium, whereas for other signs they can sometimes, psychically, be a bit unhinged. When Libras are shifted from their comfortable balance the entire world can feel like that for them, which is where peridot comes in. For a Libra who's out of sorts, it helps to restore clarity and attunement, helping to get them back on an even keel. Sometimes a Libra's superpower of seeing all sides of everything can result in indecision and lack of action. Lapis lazuli is a stone of truth and can help them to make a firm decision.

·

RECOMMENDED CRYSTALS
Opal · Peridot · Lapis Lazuli

SCORPIO

SUN SIGN DATES
23 October – 21 November

·

ELEMENT
Water

·

Scorpio is the most misunderstood sign of the zodiac. As a fixed water sign, the Scorpion hides in still depths, making Scorpios come across as mysterious and even dangerous. Topaz, whether golden or in its myriad of colours, provides insight and clarity, helping others to illuminate these depths and fathom the fathomless Scorpio. Of course, mystery can be a powerful charm, and nothing amps up Scorpio's sexy charisma like ruby, which promotes attraction and spontaneity. Meanwhile, their traditional stone of aquamarine helps them to negotiate and compromise – useful if moody, Mars-ruled Scorpio has unleashed its vicious pincers or sting!

·

RECOMMENDED CRYSTALS
Topaz · Ruby · Aquamarine

SAGITTARIUS

SUN SIGN DATES
22 November – 21 December

·

ELEMENT
Fire

·

Ruled by Jupiter, mutable fire sign Sagittarius is generally cheerful, optimistic and fun. As the Archer they're goal-oriented, but if something sends their arrow astray that jovial, chatty nature can turn cynical. Turquoise can help them to notice when this is happening and protect them from negative energies. Their blue topaz birthstone, associated with expressing truth and conscious communication, helps Sagittarius to speak effectively, useful when a thwarted Sagittarius has launched barbed conversational arrows, but also in happier moods to keep the relentlessly chatty Archer focused. Garnet helps Sagittarius to release the hidden emotional pain that a carefree, charismatic disposition can sometimes successfully conceal.

·

RECOMMENDED CRYSTALS
Blue Topaz · Turquoise · Garnet

CAPRICORN

SUN SIGN DATES
22 December – 19 January

·

ELEMENT
Earth

·

Hardworking Capricorns are the cardinal earth sign – the one with the most get-up-and-go. Being earth signs though, this manifests in a rigorous, disciplined outlook that can sometimes come across as too serious. They love their friends, but sometimes it's difficult for friends to understand Capricorn's solid intensity. Their traditional birthstone of ruby, however – once the world's most expensive stone, which suits Capricorn's high-end tastes – helps them nurture and connect with friends and partners, as well as work towards their goals. Obsidian, meanwhile, can aid in relaxation, helping Capricorns to let go of the tension their focused nature can sometimes cause them, while tiger's eye supports and channels their disciplined nature.

·

RECOMMENDED CRYSTALS
Ruby · Obsidian · Tiger's Eye

AQUARIUS

SUN SIGN DATES
20 January – 18 February

·

ELEMENT
Air

·

Aquarius can be an odd one. Often mistaken for a water sign due to being represented by the Water Carrier, its modality is fixed, which can be a confusing place for air. Aquarians, then, are unique, and their outside-the-box thinking and ability to see things slightly off-kilter makes them clever and creative. Soothing amethyst helps promote their intellect and creativity while calming their eccentric tendencies. Garnet, which like Aquarius' thoughts comes in a whole rainbow of hues, helps warm up their sometimes detached style. Traditionally ruled by Saturn, when Uranus was discovered in 1781 astrologers felt its sometimes zany energies were a better fit for Aquarius. Its associated crystal amazonite helps Aquarians connect to those higher mental powers.

·

RECOMMENDED CRYSTALS
Amethyst · Garnet · Amazonite

PISCES

SUN SIGN DATES
19 February – 20 March

·

ELEMENT
Water

·

Gentle Pisces is the last sign of the zodiac. As befits the constantly moving Fish it has a mutable modality. Traditionally ruled by Jupiter, the discovery of Neptune in 1846 prompted astrologers to assign the blue planet, named for the god of water, to this wateriest of signs. Unsurprisingly, aquamarine, once believed to hold water in its blue-green heart, is Pisceans' traditional birthstone. It helps these gentle souls face their depths and speak their truth. Pisceans tend to pour their nurturing nature out on the world; amethyst helps them keep a few drops for their own self-care. Sometimes Pisces can risk drowning in its own emotional depths, particularly when it encounters hurtful behaviour; on these occasions icy clear quartz will help them to float serenely once more.

·

RECOMMENDED CRYSTALS
Aquamarine · Amethyst · Clear Quartz

Crystal
DIVINATION

Crystals can be an invaluable tool for fortune telling, both
in their own right and in conjunction with other methods

WHAT IS DIVINATION?

Divination is the act of "divining", communicating with a
divine or supernatural force, in order to access the special
knowledge of one's fate or gain spiritual insight into a
question or situation.

Crystals and stones have enchanted and intrigued
humans for millennia, their beauty revered and their
magic put to use as jewels, charms and protective
talismans. They've been used to form monuments
like stone circles and temples, carved into relics and,
naturally, employed for soothsaying. The act of
divination with stones, precious, semi-precious or
otherwise, is known as lithomancy. There are three
common types of lithomancy: stone casting or throwing,
crystallomancy and dowsing.

Casting or throwing stones is a form of sortilege and
the method most commonly associated with the term

lithomancy. This process involves the caster tossing tumbled stones as if they were dice and interpreting where they fall in relation to each other, as well as the patterns they form.

Crystallomancy is the most prominent form of lithomancy and refers to divination that takes the form of gazing at a reflective stone, often a polished gemstone. Methods involve using the crystal as a meditative focal point or scrying.

Gemstones are also often used as a tool in dowsing. In fact, crystal dowsing is perhaps the most prevalent modern form of dowsing. They are said to be a useful source of magical energy, aiding intuition and clairvoyance. Simply incorporate them into your everyday life via jewellery, or place them upon your altar and allow their metaphysical properties to elevate your practice.

FALL IN LOVE WITH LITHOMANCY

This method of crystal fortune-telling is all about listening to your gut. Lithomancy, or stone casting, is an incredibly simple yet highly effective and insightful form of fortune telling. Stone casting involves throwing a collection of stones, held in the palm of your hand or within a small bag. It can be performed with a large number of crystals (in which case you will need a small bag) or just a few. You can toss them onto a table, the floor or even into water and interpret the ripples they create. You may also like to pay attention to the light refractions and reflections created if you are using polished or transparent stones. You needn't spend a penny on a fancy kit, you can use any crystals you may already have – your favourite clear quartz pendant, an amethyst ring or a pair of rose quartz earrings will work perfectly – although picking out a few tumble stones from your local metaphysical store is a therapeutic process, and will enable you to choose crystals that have qualities you are seeking. You'll want a set of at least ten crystals that you're familiar with in terms of what the stones represent and their properties, as this will aid you in interpreting meaning. But, the most important aspect of reading the stones is to use your intuition. As with all divination, it can be useful to cleanse your space with incense beforehand and always cleanse your crystals, simply with water or smoke!

Casting stones for love

1 Set up your circle

You may want to draw a circle using chalk or tape, lay out a cloth, use a pendulum or crystal grid or set up a space on a table. A mat or grid, particularly one that has an astrological or seasonal wheel printed onto it, will aid in your interpretation. With your eyes closed, intuitively select three crystals from your set (you may want to reach into a bag for this!) and hold them in the palm of your dominant hand.

2 Ask a question

Focus on a question, the answer of which should take into account three perspectives: your feelings, your partner's point of view and the situation. Something like "is my relationship heading for marriage?" or "is there a chance we will get back together?". Once you have decided on your question, ask it to the stones, focus and meditate on it and as you do, release your stones all at once into the circle or designated space.

3 Trust your intuition

Pay attention to where each crystal lands. The crystal that lands closest to you represents you – your motivation and true feelings. The stone central to the space or circle is the action to be taken. The third stone, neither central nor near you, represents your partner's feelings. Notice what crystals lay where – their properties and meanings. Consider where they have fallen in relation to each other and within your space, and if there are any reflections or light refractions casting off them. Pick up each one individually and get a feel for them. Does anything come immediately to mind when you touch each one? Go with your gut feeling!

"Incense can also help to centre and ground you as part of the ritual"

Predicting with pendulums

Crystal dowsing can be an invaluable tool for making decisions, as well as answering some of those burning questions

You'll need

- **A pendulum or pointed crystal attached to a single string or chain**
- **Incense or smudge stick**
- **Water**
- **Optional: pen & paper or a pendulum mat or board**

1 Pick your pendulum

A purpose-built crystal pendulum, available in most metaphysical and crystal shops or online, is the easiest and most effective way to dowse, but you could also fashion your own with a pointed crystal pendant attached to a chain or string. You can also buy metal pendulums that you can insert a crystal inside.

2 Choose the right crystal

Think about why you are dowsing and select the right crystal for your purpose. Crystals to consider to amplify and activate psychic abilities include quartz (amplifies all energies), amethyst (intuition), labradorite (destiny), lapis lazuli (self-discovery), blue apatite (psychic activation), and sodalite (intuition and insight). For questions related to love, try rose quartz or ruby in zoisite.

3 Cleanse your crystal

Wash your pendulum under running water, or use a smudge stick of dried herbs or incense to cleanse the energy of your crystal by letting the smoke drift around it. Incense can also help to centre and ground you as part of the ritual. Pick a scent like sandalwood, pine, cedarwood or sage for cleansing and intuitive clarity.

4 Get acquainted

Hold the top of the chain or string between your forefinger and thumb and let the crystal hang down straight. Keeping your hand still, ask the pendulum to show you "yes". You should see the pendulum swing either clockwise, counterclockwise, back and forth or side to side. Then ask the pendulum to show you "no" and a "maybe" and you will notice it change direction. Note its responses. You might want to try asking the crystal to show you more words or answers, it's completely up to you. Just make sure you repeat this step every time you use your pendulum.

5 Ask your questions!

Ask your pendulum a simple yes or no question and it will answer. Alternatively, you can use a mat or board or write yes and no on a piece of paper and notice the pendulum swing towards a response. You can also use your pendulum in other divination methods, for example as a way to choose which card to pick in a tarot deck. Just let your pendulum show you the way and decide your fate!

DOWSING DIVINATION

Crystal pendulums are commonly used for divination in the form of dowsing. Traditionally, pendulum dowsing was used to locate water, minerals and other valuable objects hidden beneath the ground, but dowsing with crystals can reveal much more than just a hidden hot spring. Crystal pendulums are useful for quick decision making and to enhance other divination techniques. Try using it in conjunction with the tarot to help pick out and interpret the cards. Pendulums can also be used to diagnose possible health issues. Try using one on a friend to scan their whole body to reveal energy blockages and internal issues.

Scry your heart out

Crystal gazing is one of the oldest and most popular forms of fortune-telling

Crystal gazing is a form of scrying. Also known as "seeing", it is the act of peering into a reflective surface, often in a trance-like state, until you are able to see images, interpreted as visions of prophecy. These images are often assumed to be literal moving pictures like a scene from a film, but are more often than not interpretations of shapes found inside the stone or the reflections bouncing off of its surface.

While scrying can be performed on almost anything reflective, crystal gazing is perhaps the most popular and well-known form of scrying, and is often performed using a crystal ball or an obsidian mirror.

Crystals for scrying

To begin with, pick a clear or highly reflective crystal, either made of obsidian or quartz. Obsidian has the added benefit of being grounding and protective, while quartz will amplify your physic abilities. The flat edges of a pyramid or obelisk make them easy to gaze at, but a ball's spherical nature offers a new perspective and an infinite surface.

For scrying with a crystal ball, your ball should be perfectly spherical (without a flattened base) and may be fashioned out of quartz, obsidian, beryl, calcite or even lead crystal (glass). If glass, the ball should be perfectly clear, with no air bubbles. A transparent or translucent ball enables the gazer to interpret refracted light through it. Natural crystals may contain shapes formed within its natural structure or inclusions of other minerals, which can then be interpreted.